Review, Practice, & Mastery of

COMMON CORE

MATHEMATICS

STATE STANDARDS

Reviewers

Deanna Avery • Nantucket Public Schools • Nantucket, MA

Melinda Baer • Saddleback Valley Unified School District • Lake Forest, CA

Theresa Casto • Northern Wells Community Schools • Bluffton, IN

Christine Dolan • Marlborough Public Schools • Marlborough, MA

Angela Kulacz • Elmhurst Unit School District • Elmhurst, IL

Aaron Moring-D'Angier • Cook County Schools • Chicago, IL

Bruce Rainwater • San Diego Unified • San Diego, CA

Debbie Smith • Opp City Schools • Opp, AL

Cheryl Wild • Higley Unified School District • Gilbert, AZ

© 2013 **Perfection Learning**®
www.perfectionlearning.com

4   5   6   PP   17   16   15   14   13

94652
PB ISBN: 978-0-7891-8312-5

Printed in the United States of America

To the Student

This book will help you review, practice, and master the Common Core State Standards for Mathematics. Here are the steps to follow to use this book.

1. Take the Tryout Test and check your answers. Use the chart at the bottom of this page to find out your strengths and weaknesses in the areas covered. Don't be discouraged if you don't get all the answers right or if you don't understand some questions. Remember the questions that are hard for you to answer. They will be the types of questions you need to work on the most.

2. Work through the lessons that follow the Tryout Test. Each lesson reviews example items and provides a practice test based on the Common Core State Standards. Fill in the Keeping Score chart on page 124 as you complete each practice test.

3. After completing all the lessons, take the Mastery Test. Your score on this test will show your understanding of the Common Core State Standards for Mathematics.

Unit	Tryout Test Items	Mastery Test Items
1 The Number System	1, 2, 3, 4, 5, 6, 7, 8	1, 2, 3, 4, 5, 6, 7, 8
2 Radicals and Integer Exponents	9, 10, 11, 12, 13, 14, 15	9, 10, 11, 12, 13, 14, 15
3 Proportional Relationships	16, 17, 18, 19, 20, 21, 22, 23	16, 17, 18, 19, 20, 21, 22, 23
4 Linear Equations and Systems	24, 25, 26, 27, 28, 29, 30	24, 25, 26, 27, 28, 29, 30
5 Functions	31, 32, 33, 34, 35, 36, 37	31, 32, 33, 34, 35, 36, 37
6 Geometry	38, 39, 49, 41, 42, 43, 44, 45, 46, 47	38, 39, 49, 41, 42, 43, 44, 45, 46, 47
7 The Pythagorean Theorem and Volume	48, 40, 50, 51, 52, 53	48, 40, 50, 51, 52, 53
8 Statistics	54, 55, 56, 57, 58	54, 55, 56, 57, 58

Common Core Math 8

Table of Contents

continued

Table of Contents *continued*

Tryout Test

Estimated time: 80 minutes

Directions: Read and answer each question.

1 Which number shown is closest in value to $\sqrt{315}$?

Ⓐ 18 Ⓒ 90

Ⓑ 63 Ⓓ 158

2 Kyle felt a draft of cold air. He measured a gap in a nearby window and found that it was $\frac{7}{16}$ inches wide. Which decimal is equivalent to $\frac{7}{16}$?

Ⓐ 0.23 Ⓒ 0.716

Ⓑ 0.4375 Ⓓ 2.2857

3 Between which two whole numbers is $\sqrt[3]{9}$?

Ⓐ 2 and 3 Ⓒ 7 and 8

Ⓑ 3 and 4 Ⓓ 9 and 10

4 Which shows $0.\overline{45}$ as an equivalent fraction?

Ⓐ $\frac{4}{9}$

Ⓑ $\frac{5}{9}$

Ⓒ $\frac{4}{11}$

Ⓓ $\frac{5}{11}$

5 Which of these statements is true?

Ⓐ $\frac{16}{9} < \sqrt{2}$

Ⓑ $-\frac{5}{8} < -0.75$

Ⓒ $\pi > \frac{21}{7}$

Ⓓ $\sqrt{15} > 4$

6 Which set of numbers does NOT include the square root of 25?

Ⓐ irrational numbers

Ⓑ integers

Ⓒ rational numbers

Ⓓ whole numbers

7 Which of the following is NOT a rational number?

Ⓐ $\frac{2}{3}$ Ⓒ π

Ⓑ $1\frac{1}{4}$ Ⓓ 4

8 Show that 1.7 is a rational number by writing it as the ratio of two integers.

Ⓐ $\frac{1}{17}$

Ⓑ $\frac{10}{17}$

Ⓒ $\frac{17}{10}$

Ⓓ $\frac{17}{100}$

9 Which answer choice shows 4.517×10^{-3} in standard notation?

Ⓐ 4,517 Ⓒ 0.004517

Ⓑ 1.517 Ⓓ 0.0004517

10 Find $\sqrt{169}$.

Ⓐ 23 Ⓒ 13

Ⓑ 16 Ⓓ 7

GO ON

11 What is the value of 25^2?

Ⓐ 5

Ⓑ 50

Ⓒ 252

Ⓓ 625

12 Which answer shows 0.0038 written in scientific notation?

Ⓐ 3.8×10^3

Ⓑ 3.8×10^4

Ⓒ 3.8×10^{-3}

Ⓓ 3.8×10^{-4}

13 Simplify.

$$\frac{5^3 \times 5^6}{5^{10}}$$

Ⓐ $\frac{1}{5}$

Ⓒ 5^2

Ⓑ 5

Ⓓ 5^{90}

14 $(5^4)(5^2) =$

Ⓐ 5^6

Ⓑ 5^8

Ⓒ 25^6

Ⓓ 25^8

15 The volume of a cube is 27 ft^3. What is the height of the cube?

Ⓐ 3 ft

Ⓑ 6 ft

Ⓒ 9 ft

Ⓓ 27 ft

16 What is the slope of this line?

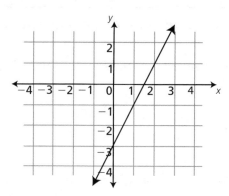

Ⓐ 2

Ⓒ $-\frac{1}{2}$

Ⓑ $\frac{1}{2}$

Ⓓ -2

17 The average speed of the tram at the amusement park is 88 yards per minute. How long will it take the tram to travel 2 miles? (1 mi = 1,760 yd)

Ⓐ 40 min

Ⓑ 44 min

Ⓒ 60 min

Ⓓ 120 min

18 Stuffed animals are on sale: 3 for $17. Margo wants to buy a stuffed animal for each of the 24 children at the day care center. Which proportion can be used to find the total cost?

Ⓐ $\frac{3}{17} = \frac{c}{24}$

Ⓑ $\frac{3}{24} = \frac{c}{24}$

Ⓒ $\frac{3}{17} = \frac{24}{c}$

Ⓓ $\frac{3}{20} = \frac{24}{c}$

19 The table shows the amount of water Jamie drinks compared to the number of miles she bikes.

Miles	Water (oz)
3	20
6	40
9	60
12	80

Which is the BEST description of the pattern?

Ⓐ Jamie drinks 3 ounces of water for every 20 miles she bikes.

Ⓑ Jamie drinks 20 ounces of water for every 3 miles she bikes.

Ⓒ Jamie drinks 20 ounces of water for every mile she bikes.

Ⓓ Jamie drinks 1 ounce of water for every 3 miles she bikes.

20 What is the equation of this line?

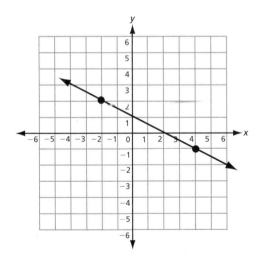

Ⓐ $y = -\frac{1}{2}x + 1$

Ⓑ $y = \frac{1}{2}x + 2$

Ⓒ $y = x + 2$

Ⓓ $y = x - 2$

21 Which is the graph for $y = -2x + 4$?

Ⓐ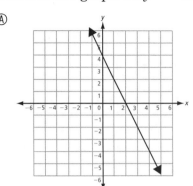

Ⓑ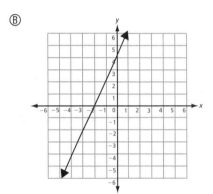

Ⓒ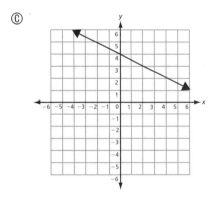

Ⓓ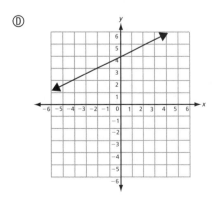

GO ON

22 What is the *y*-intercept of this graph?

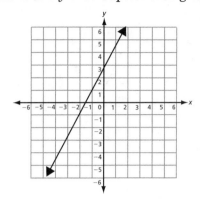

Ⓐ −1.5

Ⓑ 0

Ⓒ 3

Ⓓ 4

23 Which equation shows a line that passes through the origin?

Ⓐ $y = x + 1.5$

Ⓑ $y = x - 1.5$

Ⓒ $y = 1.5x$

Ⓓ $y = 5x + 1$

24 Find the value of *y* in the equation below.

$$\frac{y}{4} + 6 = 1$$

Ⓐ $y = 10$

Ⓑ $y = 1\frac{1}{2}$

Ⓒ $y = -1\frac{1}{2}$

Ⓓ $y = -20$

25 Solve this system by graphing.

$$2x + y = -2$$
$$3y - x = 8$$

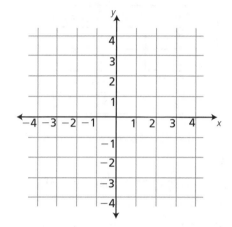

Ⓐ $(-5, 1)$ Ⓒ $(2, -6)$

Ⓑ $(-2, 2)$ Ⓓ $(2, -2)$

26 Solve $8 - 3x = 5(4 - x)$.

Ⓐ $x = -\frac{7}{2}$ Ⓒ $x = -6$

Ⓑ $x = -\frac{3}{2}$ Ⓓ $x = 6$

27 How many solutions does this equation have?

$$5 - (3 - x) = x$$

Ⓐ 0

Ⓑ 1

Ⓒ 2

Ⓓ an infinite number

28 Which ordered pair is the solution to this system of equations?

$$2x - 3y = 2$$
$$x + 2y = 8$$

Ⓐ $(-2, -4)$ Ⓒ $(2, 4)$

Ⓑ $(-2, 4)$ Ⓓ $(4, 2)$

29 Choose the system of equations that represents the problem situation below.

A rectangle is 8 inches longer than it is wide. The perimeter is 56 inches.

Ⓐ $x + 8 = y$
$x + y = 56$
Ⓑ $x + y = 8$
$x + y = 56$
Ⓒ $x + 8 = y$
$2x + 2y = 56$
Ⓓ $x + y = 8$
$x + 2y = 56$

30 A system of two linear equations has one solution. What must be true of the graphs of these equations?

Ⓐ The lines are parallel.
Ⓑ The lines are identical.
Ⓒ The line are perpendicular.
Ⓓ The lines intersect in exactly one point.

31 Which equation shows the relationship between x and y?

x	y
−1	−4
0	−1
1	2
2	5

Ⓐ $y = 3x - 1$
Ⓑ $y = 4x$
Ⓒ $y = 2x - 2$
Ⓓ $y = x - 4$

32 Which is the graph for this function?

x	−3	−2	−1	0
y	−3	−1	1	3

Ⓐ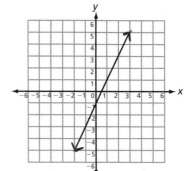

Ⓑ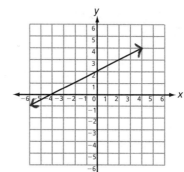

Ⓒ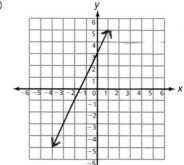

Ⓓ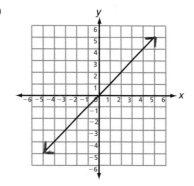

33 Which is the graph of a nonlinear function?

Ⓐ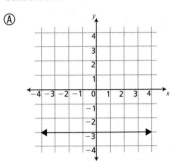

Ⓑ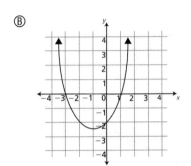

Ⓒ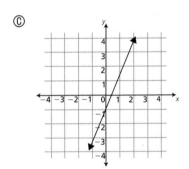

Ⓓ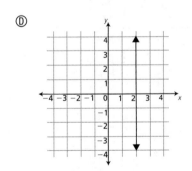

34 What relationship is shown by the ordered pairs in this table?

x	y
−1	5
0	10
−2	10
0	5

Ⓐ function that is not a relation

Ⓑ relation that is not a function

Ⓒ both a function and a relation

Ⓓ neither a function nor a relation

35 Which set of ordered pairs is not a function?

Ⓐ $\{(5, 1), (4, 1), (3, 1), (2, 1)\}$

Ⓑ $\{(5, 2), (5, 3), (5, 4), (5, 5)\}$

Ⓒ $\{(5, 5), (4, 4), (3, 3), (2, 2)\}$

Ⓓ $\{(5, 6), (4, 3), (3, 6), (2, 3)\}$

36 Carlos spent $5 for two muffins and a hot chocolate. One muffin costs twice as much as the hot chocolate. Which equation can be used to find the price of c, the hot chocolate?

Ⓐ $2(2c) + c = \$5$

Ⓑ $2c + c = \$5$

Ⓒ $(c + 2c)^2 = \$5$

Ⓓ $\frac{1}{2}c + c = \$5$

37 This graph shows a function that models the speed of a moving object. For what values of the time, x, is this function increasing?

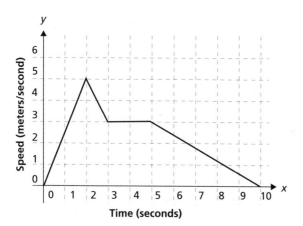

Ⓐ $0 \leq x \leq 1$ Ⓒ $2 \leq x \leq 3$

Ⓑ $0 \leq x \leq 2$ Ⓓ $3 \leq x \leq 5$

38 Plot the following points on the coordinate grid. Connect the points in order to form a quadrilateral.

$$(3, 2), (5, -3), (1, -3), (2, 2)$$

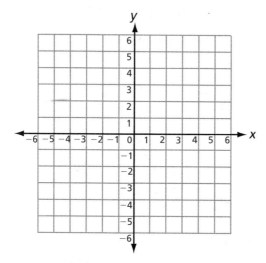

Reflect the quadrilateral over the y-axis. Which ordered pair is one of the vertices of the new figure?

Ⓐ $(2, -2)$ Ⓒ $(-3, -2)$

Ⓑ $(-5, -3)$ Ⓓ $(1, 3)$

39 If quadrilateral $KLMN$ is rotated 180° clockwise about the origin, which point will be a coordinate of the rotated figure?

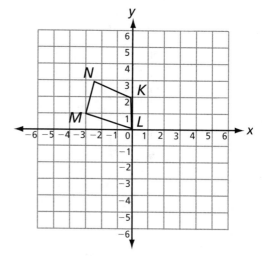

Ⓐ $(3, -1)$

Ⓑ $(-2, 3)$

Ⓒ $(0, -3)$

Ⓓ $(-1, 3)$

40 These triangles are similar.

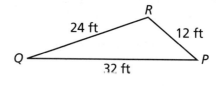

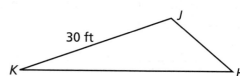

What is the length of side HK?

Ⓐ 15 ft   Ⓒ 40 ft

Ⓑ 20 ft   Ⓓ 60 ft

GO ON

41 In the figure below, *m* and *n* are parallel lines. Angle 6 has a measure of 100°. What is the measure of angle 3?

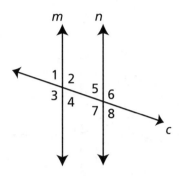

Ⓐ 260°   Ⓒ 100°

Ⓑ 180°   Ⓓ 80°

42 The vertices of triangle *PQR* are *P*(4, 8), *Q*(8, 8), and *R*(8, 2). Triangle *PQR* is reduced by a scale factor of $\frac{1}{2}$. Which are the possible coordinates of triangle *P'Q'R'*? The origin is used as the center of the dilation.

Ⓐ *P'*(3.5, 7.5), *Q'*(7.5, 7.5), *R'*(7.5, 1.5)

Ⓑ *P'*(2, 4), *Q'*(4, 4), *R'*(4, 1)

Ⓒ *P'*(2, 6), *Q'*(6, 6), *R'*(6, 0)

Ⓓ *P'*(8, 16), *Q'*(16, 16), *R'*(16, 4)

43 Figures *DFGH* and *WXYZ* are congruent. What is the measure of ∠*WZY*?

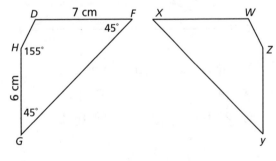

Ⓐ 45°   Ⓒ 115°

Ⓑ 65°   Ⓓ 155°

44 What is the measure of angle A?

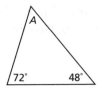

Ⓐ 240°   Ⓒ 72°

Ⓑ 120°   Ⓓ 60°

45 Which transformation is shown by this pair of figures?

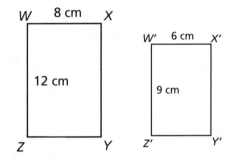

Ⓐ 180° rotation

Ⓑ horizontal translation

Ⓒ dilation by a factor of $\frac{3}{4}$

Ⓓ dilation by a factor of $\frac{4}{3}$

46 What is the measure of ∠*X* ?

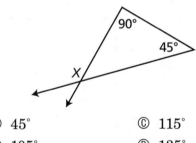

Ⓐ 45°   Ⓒ 115°

Ⓑ 105°   Ⓓ 135°

47 △ABC is reflected across the y-axis and then rotated 60° clockwise. The result is labeled △DEF. What must be true of angles A and D?

Ⓐ m∠A is twice m∠D.

Ⓑ m∠A is one-half of m∠D.

Ⓒ The angles are congruent.

Ⓓ The angles both equal 60°.

48 An ad for a computer reports the diagonal length of the screen to be 17 inches and the width of the screen to be 15 inches. What is the height of the screen?

Ⓐ 8 in.

Ⓑ 12 in.

Ⓒ 14 in.

Ⓓ 32 in.

49 A wicker basket has a diameter of 30 inches and a height of 20 inches. Which expression equals the volume of this basket?

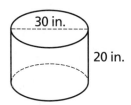

Ⓐ $\pi \times 15^2 \times 20$

Ⓑ $\pi \times 15 \times 20^2$

Ⓒ $\pi \times 30^2 \times 20$

Ⓓ $\pi \times 30 \times 20^2$

50 Jill took a photograph of a plane taking off. Her mother is an air-traffic controller and was able to estimate the measurements shown. How far is the plane above the ground? Round to the nearest yard.

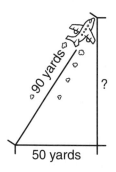

Ⓐ 75 yards

Ⓑ 60 yards

Ⓒ 56 yards

Ⓓ 40 yards

51 Georgia designed a home in the shape of a cone for a futuristic homes project. The diagram shows the measurements she envisioned for the actual home. Find the volume of the home. Round to the nearest foot. (Use 3.14 for π.)

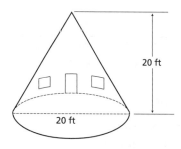

Ⓐ 8,373 ft³

Ⓑ 6,280 ft³

Ⓒ 2,093 ft³

Ⓓ 1,256 ft³

GO ON

52 Which set of measurements can be used to make a right triangle?

Ⓐ 6 cm, 8 cm, 9 cm

Ⓑ 9 cm, 12 cm, 15 cm

Ⓒ 12 cm, 30 cm, 35 cm

Ⓓ 20 cm, 21 cm, 28 cm

53 What is the distance from point P at $(-20, 4)$ to point Q at $(15, -8)$?

Answer: _____

54 The scatterplot below shows data Tina collected. She compared the number of newspapers she delivered to the amount of time it took her to deliver them. What is the relationship between the two sets of data?

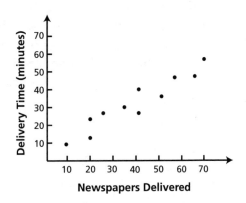

Ⓐ strong positive

Ⓑ strong negative

Ⓒ weak negative

Ⓓ none

55 Which is the line of best fit for the data shown on this graph?

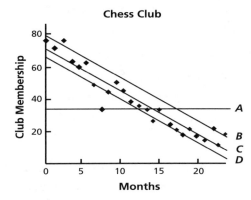

Ⓐ line A Ⓒ line C

Ⓑ line B Ⓓ line D

56 The scatterplot shows the number of sheets of paper Adam had left at the end of each week.

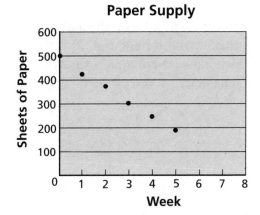

According to the scatterplot, when will Adam run out of paper?

Ⓐ week 6

Ⓑ week 7

Ⓒ week 8

Ⓓ week 9

57 What relationship is suggested by this scatterplot?

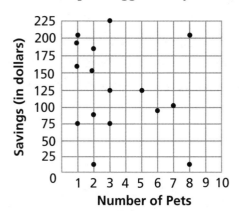

Ⓐ People with more pets save more.

Ⓑ People with more pets save less.

Ⓒ People who save the most have the fewest pets.

Ⓓ The number of pets is not related to the amount saved.

58 Madge kept track of the sales at her sportswear store. Here is her data.

Sportswear Sales
S = small   L = large
M = medium   X = extra large
T-shirts   L L S X L S S L L M M
X L L S S S X M L X L
Polos   S S L S L M M M X M X
L L M M M X S X M L S
Hoodies   M M L M S X L X X L S
L S X M S S L X M M L

Madge used a two-way table to organize her data. Which is the missing number in her table?

	S	M	L	X
T-shirts	6	3	9	4
Polos	5	8	5	4
Hoodies	5	6	?	5

Ⓐ 4   Ⓒ 6

Ⓑ 5   Ⓓ 8

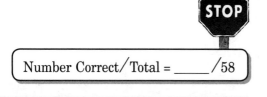

Number Correct/Total = _____/58

The Number System

Directions: Read and answer each question.

Rational Numbers

1 Show that 2.5 is a rational number by writing it as a ratio of two integers.

    Ⓐ $\frac{2}{5}$ Ⓒ $\frac{3}{2}$

    Ⓑ $\frac{2.5}{1}$ Ⓓ $\frac{5}{2}$

Think It Through

To answer **example 1**, first rewrite 2.5 as a mixed number.

$$2.5 = 2\frac{1}{2}$$

Convert the mixed number into an improper fraction.

$$2\frac{1}{2} = \boxed{}$$

Remember . . .

A ratio is a comparison of two numbers through division.

$$\frac{4}{3} = \text{the ratio 4 to 3}$$

2 Which number is NOT a rational number?

 Ⓐ $\frac{5}{8}$ Ⓒ 0.714714 . . .

 Ⓑ -3 Ⓓ π

Examples of Rational Numbers

Integers:

$$-20 = -\frac{20}{1} \qquad 0 = \frac{0}{1} \qquad 6 = \frac{6}{1}$$

Fractions:

$$5\frac{1}{3} = \frac{16}{3} \quad -0.25 = -\frac{1}{4} \quad 0.75 = \frac{3}{4}$$

Decimals:

$$-0.5 = -\frac{1}{2} \quad 4.7 = \frac{47}{10} \quad 0.45 = \frac{9}{20}$$

$$0.8\overline{3} \ldots = \frac{5}{6}$$

3 Which is an irrational number?

 Ⓐ $\sqrt{16}$

 Ⓑ $\sqrt{100}$

 Ⓒ $\sqrt{50}$

 Ⓓ $\sqrt{81}$

Irrational Numbers

Irrational numbers cannot be written in the form a/b, where a and b are integers and $b \neq 0$. Examples of irrational numbers are square roots that are not square numbers, such as $\sqrt{3}$, and nonrepeating, nonterminating decimals such as π.

Step-By-Step

To answer **example 2**, look at each answer choice. Which choice cannot be written as a fraction?

1 Choice Ⓐ is a fraction, so it is a rational number.

2 Write choice Ⓑ as a fraction.

3 Choice Ⓒ is a repeating decimal. All repeating decimals are rational numbers.

4 Choice Ⓓ is π. When the value of π is written, it is a decimal that continues forever with no repeating pattern. π is called an **irrational number** since it cannot be written as a fraction. The fraction $\frac{22}{7}$ is an approximation of π.

Step-By-Step

To solve **example 3**, look for the number under the square root sign that is not a perfect square.

1 $4^2 = 4 \times 4 =$ _____

 $10^2 = 10 \times 10 =$ _____

 $9^2 = 9 \times 9 =$ _____

2 The square root of 50 is an irrational number. The correct answer is choice _____.

GO ON

Irrational Numbers

4 Which is an irrational number?

Ⓐ 0.666 . . .

Ⓑ 0.454545 . . .

Ⓒ 0.123123123 . . .

Ⓓ 0.12122122212222 . . .

Step-By-Step

Remember that a decimal that does not terminate or eventually repeat is an irrational number. Look for the repeating digits in each answer to find the irrational number.

1 Choice Ⓐ: the digit _____

Choice Ⓑ: the digits _____

Choice Ⓒ: the digits _____

2 The decimal that has no repeating pattern is the one in answer choice _____.

5 Which is an irrational number?

Ⓐ $\sqrt{25}$ Ⓒ $0.\overline{123}$

Ⓑ $\sqrt{51.84}$ Ⓓ $\sqrt{2}$

Rational and Irrational Numbers

Rational numbers are numbers that can be written as either a fraction or a decimal that terminates or repeats.

Examples of rational numbers are:

25, 4.626, $\frac{3}{4}$, $-6\frac{1}{2}$, and $0.\overline{72}$.

Irrational numbers are unending, never-repeating decimals.

Pi (π) is an example of an irrational number. Here are the first twenty digits of pi.

3.1415926535897932384 . . .

We use $\frac{22}{7}$, or 3.14, as a rational approximation of π.

Step-By-Step

Evaluate each answer choice in **example 5** to determine if it is rational.

1 Evaluate answer Ⓐ by simplifying $\sqrt{25}$.

$$\sqrt{25} = \boxed{}$$

$\sqrt{25}$ is rational since 5 can be written as the fraction $\frac{5}{1}$.

2 Evaluate answer Ⓑ by simplifying $\sqrt{51.84}$. You know the square root of 51.84 will be close to 7 since 7^2 is 49. Guess and check until you find the correct answer.

$$\sqrt{51.84} = 7.2$$

$\sqrt{51.84}$ is rational since 7.2 is a decimal that terminates.

3 Evaluate answer Ⓒ. The number $0.\overline{123}$ is a repeating decimal, so it is rational.

4 $\sqrt{2}$ is an unending, never-repeating decimal. That makes it an irrational number.

$$\sqrt{2} = 1.41421356 . . .$$

6 Write $0.\overline{54}$ as a fraction.

Answer: _____

Converting Repeating Decimals

Count the number of digits that repeat. Multiply both sides of the equation by 10 to that power.

$0.\overline{6}$ (1 digit repeats) $\longrightarrow$ multiply by 10^1

$0.\overline{54}$ (2 digits repeat) $\longrightarrow$ multiply by 10^2

$4.\overline{372}$ (3 digits repeat) $\longrightarrow$ multiply by 10^3

x digits repeat $\longrightarrow$ multiply by 10^x

Benchmarks

Memorize these benchmark repeating decimals and equivalent fractions.

Fraction	Decimal
$\frac{1}{3}$	0.333 . . .
$\frac{2}{3}$	0.666 . . .
$\frac{1}{6}$	0.1666 . . .
$\frac{1}{9}$	0.111 . . .
$\frac{1}{11}$	0.090909 . . .
$\frac{1}{12}$	0.08333 . . .

Step-By-Step

In **example 6**, the bar above the 54 in $0.\overline{54}$ indicates that $0.\overline{54}$ is a **repeating decimal**. In a repeating decimal, the numbers under the bar repeat endlessly.

1 Set $0.\overline{54}$ equal to n. Since two digits repeat, show two groups of the repeating digits.

$$n = 0.\overline{54}$$

$$n = 0.54\overline{54}$$

2 Multiply both sides of the equation by 10^2. This step will move the first set of repeating digits to the left of the decimal point.

$$n \times 100 = 0.54\overline{54} \times 100$$

$$100n = 54.\overline{54}$$

3 Subtract the original equation from the new equation to cancel out the repeating portions.

$$100n = 54.\overline{54}$$
$$-\quad n = \quad 0.\overline{54}$$
$$\overline{99n = 54}$$

4 Solve for n to get a fraction.

$$99n = 54$$

$$n = \frac{54}{99}$$

5 Write the fraction in its simplest form. (Hint: Divide the numerator and denominator by 9.)

$$0.\overline{54} = \frac{54}{99} \div \frac{9}{9} = \boxed{}$$

Approximating Irrational Numbers

7 Which whole number is closest to the value of $\sqrt{193}$?

Answer: _____

8 Which is the best estimate of $\sqrt[3]{30}$?

    Ⓐ 2   Ⓒ 4

    Ⓑ 3   Ⓓ 5

Real Numbers

Together, the rational and irrational numbers make up the real numbers.

1 Which set of numbers includes the square root of 42?

   Ⓐ irrational numbers

   Ⓑ integers

   Ⓒ rational numbers

   Ⓓ whole numbers

2 What is the name of this set?

$$\{\ldots -3, -2, -1, 0, 1, 2, 3, \ldots\}$$

   Ⓐ real numbers

   Ⓑ integers

   Ⓒ rational numbers

   Ⓓ whole numbers

3 Which set does not include negative numbers?

   Ⓐ real numbers

   Ⓑ integers

   Ⓒ rational numbers

   Ⓓ whole numbers

4 Which of these equals an integer?

   Ⓐ $12 \div 5$ Ⓒ $-15 \div 4$

   Ⓑ $-12 \div 5$ Ⓓ $-15 \div 5$

5 Which of these is closest to $\sqrt{150}$?

   Ⓐ 12.2   Ⓒ 14.2

   Ⓑ 12.4   Ⓓ 15

6 $3.24\overline{55}$ is what kind of number?

   Ⓐ rational, real

   Ⓑ irrational, real

   Ⓒ integer, rational

   Ⓓ whole number, rational

7 Write $0.\overline{72}$ as a fraction.

   Answer: _____

8 Which is the best estimate of the $\sqrt[3]{81}$

   Answer: _____

GO ON

Comparing Rational and Irrational Numbers

9 Which point on the number line is closest to $\sqrt{70}$?

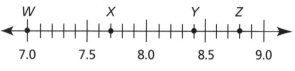

W   X   Y   Z

7.0   7.5   8.0   8.5   9.0

   Ⓐ point W Ⓒ point Y

   Ⓑ point X Ⓓ point Z

Think It Through

When answering **example 9**, remember that any square root can be located on a number line.

You can eliminate choices Ⓐ and Ⓑ because $\sqrt{70}$ must be greater than 8. Square 8.4 and 8.8 and choose the one that is closer to 70.

$$8.4^2 = \boxed{}$$

$$8.8^2 = \boxed{}$$

---

10 Which statement is true?

   Ⓐ $\sqrt{7} > 2.8$

   Ⓑ $-3/4 < -0.7\overline{1}$

   Ⓒ $\pi > 3.1\overline{4}$

   Ⓓ $3 > \sqrt{10}$

Think It Through

Write each of the numbers in **example 10** as a decimal and compare the numbers. Then decide which answer is correct.

$$\sqrt{7} > 2.8$$

$$2.64 \ldots \boxed{} \; 2.8$$

$$-\frac{3}{4} < -0.7\overline{1}$$

$$-0.75 \boxed{} \; -0.7\overline{1}$$

$$\pi > 3.1\overline{4}$$

$$3.14159 \ldots \boxed{} \; 3.1\overline{4}$$

$$3 > \sqrt{10}$$

$$3 \boxed{} \; 3.16 \ldots$$

Go for it!

Test Practice 1: The Number System

Estimated time: 20 minutes

Directions: Read and answer each question.

1 Which set of numbers includes the square root of 20?

Ⓐ irrational numbers
Ⓑ integers
Ⓒ rational numbers
Ⓓ whole numbers

2 Which number is an irrational number?

Ⓐ $4\frac{5}{6}$
Ⓒ $0.15783623\ldots$
Ⓑ -11
Ⓓ $2.35858585\ldots$

3 Which of these is a rational number?

Ⓐ $\sqrt{8}$
Ⓒ $\sqrt{30}$
Ⓑ $\sqrt{25}$
Ⓓ π

4 Which is an irrational number?

Ⓐ $\sqrt{81}$
Ⓒ $\sqrt{5}$
Ⓑ -11
Ⓓ $0.\overline{3}$

5 Which choice orders the numbers from least to greatest?

Ⓐ $2.\overline{22},\ \sqrt{5},\ 2\frac{3}{5},\ 2\frac{5}{8}$
Ⓑ $2\frac{5}{8},\ 2\frac{3}{5},\ 2.\overline{22},\ \sqrt{5}$
Ⓒ $2\frac{5}{8},\ 2\frac{3}{5},\ \sqrt{5},\ 2.\overline{22}$
Ⓓ $2.\overline{22},\ 2\frac{3}{5},\ 2\frac{5}{8},\ \sqrt{5}$

6 Between which two whole numbers is $\sqrt{456}$?

Ⓐ 20 and 21
Ⓑ 21 and 22
Ⓒ 22 and 23
Ⓓ 23 and 24

7 Which square root is marked as a point on this number line?

Ⓐ $\sqrt{-3}$
Ⓒ $\sqrt{2.5}$
Ⓑ $\sqrt{0.5}$
Ⓓ $\sqrt{5}$

8 $\sqrt{175} \approx$

Ⓐ between 12 and 13
Ⓑ between 13 and 14
Ⓒ between 14 and 15
Ⓓ 14.1

9 Between which two whole numbers is $\sqrt{227}$?

Ⓐ 20 and 21
Ⓑ 15 and 16
Ⓒ 13 and 14
Ⓓ 11 and 12

10 Which number is greater than $\frac{7}{2}$?

Ⓐ $\sqrt[3]{27}$
Ⓑ $\sqrt{13}$
Ⓒ $3.\overline{4}$
Ⓓ π

11 Which symbol makes this number sentence true?

$$\pi \ \Box \ \sqrt{4}$$

Ⓐ $<$　　Ⓒ $=$

Ⓑ $>$　　Ⓓ $\leq$

12 Which answer lists the numbers from greatest to least?

Ⓐ $\frac{6}{11}$, 1.015, $\sqrt{3}$, $\sqrt[3]{8}$

Ⓑ $\sqrt{3}$, $\sqrt[3]{8}$, 1.015, $\frac{6}{11}$

Ⓒ $\sqrt[3]{8}$, $\sqrt{3}$, 1.015, $\frac{6}{11}$

Ⓓ $\sqrt[3]{8}$, $\frac{6}{11}$, 1.015, $\sqrt{3}$

13 Between which two whole numbers is $\sqrt[3]{83}$?

Ⓐ 4 and 5　　Ⓒ 8 and 9

Ⓑ 6 and 7　　Ⓓ 9 and 10

14 Which whole number is closest to $\sqrt{355}$?

Answer: _____

DIRECTIONS FOR QUESTION 15: Respond fully to the open-ended question that follows. Show your work and clearly explain your answer. Write your answer in the space below.

15 Write $0.\overline{123}$ as an equivalent fraction.

Answer: _____

Explanation: _____

_____

_____

_____

Number Correct/Total = _____ /15

24

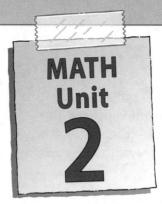

MATH Unit 2

Radicals and Integer Exponents

1 Exponential Expressions **[8.EE.1]**
2 Properties of Integer Exponents **[8.EE.1]**
3 Squares and Square Roots **[8.EE.2]**
4 Cubes and Cube Roots **[8.EE.2]**
5 Scientific Notation for Large Numbers **[8.EE.3, 8.EE.4]**
6 Scientific Notation for Small Numbers **[8.EE.4]**

Directions: Read and answer each question.

Exponential Expressions

1 Which is equivalent to 4^5?

  Ⓐ 9   Ⓒ 625
  Ⓑ 20   Ⓓ 1,024

2 Which shows $8 \times 8 \times 8 \times 8$ in exponential form?

  Ⓐ 8^4 Ⓒ 4^8
  Ⓑ 8^8 Ⓓ 4^4

Step-By-Step

In **example 1**, the exponent tells you how many times the base is used as a factor.

1 4^5 is read *the fifth power of 4* or *4 to the fifth power*. The *base* is 4. The *exponent* is 5.

2 Write 4 as a factor 5 times. Then simplify.

$$4 \times 4 \times 4 \times 4 \times 4 = \boxed{}$$

Think It Through

For **example 2**, the product can be written in exponential form with a base of 8 and an exponent of 4.

$$8 \times 8 \times 8 \times 8 = 8^4$$

GO ON →

3 Which shows 2^{-6} as a fraction?

Ⓐ $-\frac{2}{6}$ Ⓒ $\frac{1}{2}6$

Ⓑ $\frac{1}{10}6$ Ⓓ $\frac{1}{12}$

Remember . . .

$2^4 = 2 \times 2 \times 2 \times 2 = 16$

$2^{-4} = 1 \div (2 \times 2 \times 2 \times 2) = \frac{1}{2^4} = \frac{1}{16}$

4 Simplify this expression.

$$(4^3)^2$$

Ⓐ 4^6 Ⓒ 4^1

Ⓑ 4^5 Ⓓ 4^9

Step-By-Step

To answer **example 3**, you must realize that a negative exponent converts into a fraction with 1 as the numerator. The denominator is the base with the positive exponent.

1 Write 1 as the numerator of a fraction.

2 Change the exponent to a positive number and write the new expression as the denominator. Which answer choice shows this expression?

Step-By-Step

The expression in **example 4** can be written as a multiplication expression.

1 $(4^3)^2$ is the square of 4^3.

$$(4^3)^2 = 4^3 \times 4^3 = 4 \times 4 \times 4 \times 4 \times 4 \times 4$$
$$= 4^6$$

2 The "Power of a Power" rule found in the *Rules for Exponents* table shows another way to simplify $(4^3)^2$.

$$(4^3)^2 = 4^{3 \times 2} = 4^6$$

Rules for Exponents

For all real numbers a, b, m, and n—

	Rule	**Example**
Power of 1	$a^1 = a$	$2^1 = 2$
Power of 0	$a^0 = 1$	$2^0 = 1$
Negative powers	$a^{-m} = \frac{1}{a^m}$	$2^{-4} = \frac{1}{2^4}$
Product of powers	$a^m \times a^n = a^{m+n}$	$2^4 \times 2^2 = 2^{4+2} = 2^6$
Quotient of powers	$a^m \div a^n = a^{m-n}$	$2^4 \div 2^2 = 2^{4-2} = 2^2$
Power of a power	$(a^m)^n = a^{m \times n}$	$(2^4)^2 = 2^{4 \times 2} = 2^8$
Power of a product	$(ab)^m = a^m \times b^m$	$(2 \times 4)^4 = 2^4 \times 4^4$

5 Which answer shows the expression in simplest form?

$$5^4 \times 5^5$$

Ⓐ 25^{20} Ⓒ 9^5

Ⓑ 5^9 Ⓓ 5

Step-By-Step

Use the *Rules for Exponents* box to evaluate expressions involving exponents, as in **example 5**.

1 Decide which rule to use. The "Product of Powers" rule states that you can multiply powers with the same base by adding the exponents.

2 Add the exponents to simplify the expression.

$$5^4 \times 5^5 = 5^{(4+5)} = 5\,\rule{1.2em}{0pt}$$

---

6 Which shows this expression in simplest form?

$$\frac{5^2 \times 5^3}{5^7}$$

Ⓐ $\frac{1}{25}$ Ⓒ 5

Ⓑ $\frac{1}{5}$ Ⓓ 125

Step-By-Step

Use the *Laws of Exponents* box to answer **example 6**.

1 Simplify the numerator by following the law for the product of powers.

$$\frac{5^2 \times 5^3}{5^7} = \frac{5^{2+3}}{5^7} = \frac{5^5}{5^7}$$

2 Use the law for the quotient of powers to simplify.

$$\frac{5^5}{5^7} = 5^5 \div 5^7 = 5^{5-7} = 5^{-2} = \frac{1}{5^2}$$

3 Check your answer by expanding the expression. Write each exponent in expanded form and cancel the factors in the numerator and denominator.

$$\frac{5^5}{5^7} = \frac{\cancel{5} \times \cancel{5} \times \cancel{5} \times \cancel{5} \times \cancel{5}}{\cancel{5} \times \cancel{5} \times \cancel{5} \times \cancel{5} \times \cancel{5} \times 5 \times 5} = \frac{1}{5^2}$$

GO ON

Questions 1–3: Write each expression as a fraction. Do not simplify the exponent.

1 9^{-4} _____

2 6^{-6} _____

3 4^{-10} _____

Questions 4–6: Write each expression as a fraction in simplest form.

4 2^{-3} _____

5 10^{-4} _____

6 4^{-4} _____

Questions 7–10: Write each expression in exponential form.

7 $\dfrac{1}{(5 \times 5 \times 5 \times 5)}$ _____

8 $9 \times 9 \times 9 \times 9 \times 9 \times 9$ _____

9 $\dfrac{1}{(10 \times 10 \times 10 \times 10 \times 10)}$ _____

10 $\dfrac{10}{(3 \times 3 \times 3 \times 3 \times 3 \times 3)}$ _____

Questions 11–13: Write each expression in simplest exponential form.

11 $3^6 \times 3^2$ _____

12 $2^8 \div 2^2$ _____

13 $(4^3 \times 4^2) \div (4^6 \times 4^3)$ _____

14 Which expression shows 7^{-2} in simplified fraction form?

Ⓐ -49 Ⓒ $-\frac{1}{14}$

Ⓑ -14 Ⓓ $\frac{1}{49}$

15 Which shows an equivalent expression?

$$8 \times \frac{4^3 \times 4^6}{4^8}$$

Ⓐ 1 Ⓒ 32

Ⓑ 8 Ⓓ 64

16 Which shows an equivalent expression?

$$(5^3 \times 5^7) \times 5^{-8}$$

Ⓐ 5^{27} Ⓒ 5

Ⓑ 5^2 Ⓓ $\frac{1}{5}$

Squares and Square Roots

7 Which number is $\sqrt{144}$?

   Ⓐ 11   Ⓒ 14

   Ⓑ 12   Ⓓ 20,738

8 Which of the following is equal to a whole number?

   Ⓐ $\sqrt{181}$ Ⓒ $\sqrt{560}$

   Ⓑ $\sqrt{361}$ Ⓓ $\sqrt{735}$

Squares and Square Roots

The square of a given number is the product of the number multiplied by itself.

$$5^2 = 5 \times 5 = 25$$

$$(-5)^2 = (-5) \times (-5) = 25$$

The square root of a number is a number that when multiplied by itself equals the given number.

$$\sqrt{25} = 5 \text{ or } -5$$

Here are two other ways to show that 25 has two different square roots.

$$\sqrt{25} = \{5, -5\}$$

$$\sqrt{25} = \pm 5$$

The brackets { } are used to show any set of numbers. The $\pm$ means "plus or minus."

Finding square roots and squaring a number are inverse operations.

Think It Through

The radical sign, $\sqrt{}$ in **example 7** means square root. To find the square root of 144, look for a number that when multiplied by itself gives 144.

   Try 11: $11 \times 11 = 121$

   That is not enough.

   Try 12: $12 \times 12 = 144$

   $\sqrt{144} = $ ⬚

Think It Through

Example 8 asks you to find the perfect square. A *perfect square* is a number whose square root is an integer or quotient of integers. Find the answer choice whose value is a whole number.

$\sqrt{181} = $ ⬚ $\sqrt{560} = $ ⬚

$\sqrt{361} = $ ⬚ $\sqrt{735} = $ ⬚

Remember . . .

Finding the square root of a number is NOT the same as dividing by 2. You are looking for a number that when multiplied by itself has a product of the given number.

   $\sqrt{9} = 3$ because $3 \times 3 = 9$.

   $\sqrt{100} = 10$ because $10 \times 10 = 100$.

GO ON

Squares and Square Roots

9 The area of a square is 100 square meters. What is the perimeter of the square?

Answer: _____

Step-By-Step

To find the length of the square's sides in **example 9**, you must find the square root of the area.

1 The formula for the area of a square is $A = s^2$. Replace A with 100.

$$A = s^2$$
$$100 = s^2$$

2 What number s when multiplied by itself is 100?

$10 \times 10 = 100$ and $-10 \times -10 = 100$

3 Length cannot be negative, so s must equal 10.

4 The formula for the perimeter of a square is $P = 4s$. Replace s with 10.

$$P = 4s$$
$$P = 4 \times 10 = \boxed{} \text{ meters}$$

Cubes and Cube Roots

10 Find the value of $\sqrt[3]{27}$.

Ⓐ 9   Ⓒ 3

Ⓑ 6   Ⓓ $\frac{1}{9}$

Cubes and Cube Roots

The **cube** of a given number is the product of the number multiplied by itself three times.

$$5^3 = 5 \times 5 \times 5 = 125$$

The **cube root** of a given number is a number that when multiplied by itself three times equals the given number.

$5 \times 5 \times 5 = 125$, so $\sqrt[3]{125} = 5$

Step-By-Step

In **example 10**, $\sqrt[3]{27}$ means the *cube root of 27*. Follow these steps to find the answer.

1 Think of a number that equals 27 when cubed or taken to the power of 3.

$$n^3 = 27$$
$$n \times n \times n = 27$$
$$\boxed{} \times \boxed{} \times \boxed{} = 27$$

Cubes and Cube Roots

11 The volume of a cube is 27 yd^3. What is the length of one edge of the cube?

Answer: _____

Try It

17 What is the value of $\sqrt{169}$?

Ⓐ −13 Ⓒ −169

Ⓑ 13 or −13 Ⓓ 13

18 If $z^2 = 169$, $z =$

Ⓐ −13 Ⓒ −169

Ⓑ 13 or −13 Ⓓ 13

19 The volume of a cube is 64 yd^3. What is the length of one edge of the cube?

Answer: _____

Scientific Notation for Large Numbers

12 What is the standard form of 2.6×10^3?

Ⓐ 0.0026 Ⓒ 2,600

Ⓑ 260 Ⓓ 26,000

Remember . . .

Scientific notation shows the product of a number between 1 and 10 and a power of 10. Scientific notation is useful for expressing very small and very large numbers.

Step-By-Step

Find the cube root of the volume to solve **example 11**.

1 The formula for the volume of a cube is $V = s^3$. Replace V with 27.

$$27 = s^3$$

2 What number s multiplied by itself three times equals 27?

$$3 \times 3 \times 3 = 27$$

3 The cube root of 27 is 3. Each edge of the cube must be 3 yards long.

Step-By-Step

Example 12 asks you to read a number in scientific notation.

1 Find the value of 10^3.

$$10^3 = 10 \times 10 \times 10 = \boxed{}$$

2 Multiply by 2.6.

$$2.6 \times 1,000 = \boxed{}$$

GO ON

Scientific Notation for Large Numbers

13 What is 3,275,000 written in scientific notation?

　ⓐ 32.75×10^3

　ⓑ 3.275×10^4

　ⓒ 3.275×10^5

　ⓓ 3.275×10^6

14 What is 2.675×10^4 written in standard form?

Answer: _____

Scientific Notation for Small Numbers

15 Which answer shows 0.000409 written in scientific notation?

Ⓐ 4.09×10^{-4} Ⓒ 4.09×10^{-3}

Ⓑ 4.09×10^{4} Ⓓ 4.9×10

Scientific Notation

Scientific notation is used to make very large and very small numbers easier to read.

$$5{,}700{,}000 = 5.7 \times 1{,}000{,}000 =$$
$$5.7 \times 10^{6}$$

$$0.000023 = 2.3 \times \tfrac{1}{100000} =$$
$$2.3 \times 10^{-5}$$

16 One day is about 0.00274 of a year. How is this number expressed in scientific notation?

Ⓐ 2.74×10^{3}

Ⓑ 2.74×10^{-2}

Ⓒ 2.74×10^{-3}

Ⓓ 2.74×10^{-4}

Remember . . .

A positive exponent tells you to move the decimal point to the right.

$$1.5 \times 10^{2} = 150$$

A negative exponent tells you to move the decimal point to the left.

$$1.5 \times 10^{-2} = 0.015$$

Step-By-Step

To convert the number in **example 15** to scientific notation, write it as a number between 1 and 10 multiplied by a power of 10.

1 Move the decimal to make a number between 1 and 10.

2 Count the number of places you moved the decimal.

$$0.000409$$
$$1\;2\;3\;4$$

3 The number of places you move the decimal is the value of the exponent of 10. If you move the decimal to the right, the value is negative; if you move it to the left, the value is positive.

4 Write the second part of the scientific notation.

$$4.09 \times \boxed{}$$

Step-By-Step

1 To write the number in **example 16** in scientific notation, first move the decimal point to the right until you have created a number between 1 and 10.

2 Next, count the number of places you moved the decimal point. This is the exponent on 10. The exponent is negative if the original decimal is less than 1.

$$0.00274 = 2.74 \times \boxed{}$$

Questions 20–22: Write the standard form of each number.

20 6.03×10^3 _____

21 2.109×10^{-6} _____

22 8.915×10^{10} _____

Questions 23–24: Write each number in scientific notation.

23 0.000006035 _____

24 $98,605,000,000$ _____

25 Which number is greater than 5.65×10^{-4} but less than 0.0006?

   Ⓐ 0.00561   Ⓒ 0.0065239

   Ⓑ 0.0009017   Ⓓ 0.000581

Go for it!

Test Practice 2: Radicals and Integer Exponents Estimated time: 20 minutes

Directions: Read and answer each question.

1 What is the value of $\sqrt{81}$?

    Ⓐ 0.81   Ⓒ $\frac{1}{9}$

    Ⓑ 9   Ⓓ 40.5

2 Which number is a perfect square?

    Ⓐ 600   Ⓒ 238

    Ⓑ 529   Ⓓ 156

3 Which shows 0.0000519 expressed in scientific notation?

    Ⓐ 5.19×10^{-5}

    Ⓑ 5.19×10^{5}

    Ⓒ 51.9×10^{-4}

    Ⓓ 51.9×10^{4}

4 What is the value of $\sqrt[3]{64}$?

    Answer: _____

5 Which shows another way to write $6 \times 6 \times 6 \times 6 \times 6$?

    Ⓐ 6^{5} Ⓒ 6^{6}

    Ⓑ 5^{6} Ⓓ 5^{5}

6 What standard number is represented by 3.8×10^{5}?

    Ⓐ 3,800

    Ⓑ 38,000

    Ⓒ 380,000

    Ⓓ 3,800,000

7 Which shows 0.00000464 expressed in scientific notation?

    Ⓐ 46.4×10^{-5}

    Ⓑ 4.64×10^{6}

    Ⓒ 4.64×10^{-6}

    Ⓓ 4.64×10^{5}

8 What is the value of 3^{-2}?

    Ⓐ -32 Ⓒ 1

    Ⓑ -6 Ⓓ $\frac{1}{9}$

9 What is 2.48×10^{3} written in standard notation?

    Answer: _____

10 What is the value of 2^{-4}?

    Ⓐ -8 Ⓒ $\frac{1}{8}$

    Ⓑ -16 Ⓓ $\frac{1}{16}$

11 Which number is NOT a perfect square?

    Ⓐ 81   Ⓒ 121

    Ⓑ 111   Ⓓ 225

12 Which number is $\sqrt{441}$?

    Ⓐ 20.1   Ⓒ 41

    Ⓑ 21   Ⓓ 44

13 $(4 + 2)^{3} \times (6^{4})^{2} =$

    Ⓐ 6^{9} Ⓒ 6^{24}

    Ⓑ 6^{11} Ⓓ 3^{68}

GO ON

14 $20 - 3^2 =$

  Ⓐ 11   Ⓒ 169

  Ⓑ 14   Ⓓ 289

15 The top of a square table has an area of 256 square inches. What is the length of each side of the table?

  Ⓐ 16 inches   Ⓒ 36 inches

  Ⓑ 26 inches   Ⓓ 65,636 inches

16 The volume of a cube is 125 cm^3. What is the length of one edge of the cube?

  Ⓐ 5 cm   Ⓒ 41.7 cm

  Ⓑ 15 cm   Ⓓ 62.5 cm

17 Write 402,000,000 in scientific notation.

  Answer: _____

18 Simplify this expression.

  $$(9^2 \times 9^6) \div (9^4 \times 9^2)$$

  Answer: _____

19 $(2^4)^5 =$

  Answer: _____

20 Which shows an equivalent expression?

  $$\frac{8^6 \times 8^3 \times 8^5}{8^9 \times 8^6}$$

  Ⓐ $\frac{8^{90}}{8^{54}}$ Ⓒ 1

  Ⓑ 7   Ⓓ $\frac{1}{8}$

Number Correct / Total = _____ / 20

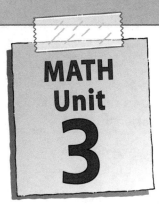

MATH Unit 3

Proportional Relationships

1 The Unit Rate **[8.EE.5]**
2 Proportional Relationships **[8.EE.5]**
3 Comparing Proportional Relationships **[8.EE.5]**
4 Slope **[8.EE.6]**
5 Equations for Lines **[8.EE.6]**

Directions: Read and answer each question.

The Unit Rate

1 Shelly ran 2 miles in 30 minutes. Which shows how fast Shelly ran in miles per hour?

Ⓐ 1 mile per hour

Ⓑ 4 miles per hour

Ⓒ $8\frac{1}{2}$ miles per hour

Ⓓ 15 miles per hour

Rate and Unit Rate

A rate is a ratio that compares two quantities with different units of measure.

2 miles / 0.5 hour

A unit rate is a rate that has a unit of 1 as its second term.

4 miles / 1 hour

Step-By-Step

Follow these steps to solve **example 1**.

1 Convert 30 minutes into hours.

30 minutes = ☐ hour

2 Write a ratio comparing the distance Shelly ran to the time in hours it took her to run the distance.

$$\frac{\boxed{} \text{ miles}}{0.5 \text{ hour}}$$

3 Multiply the numerator and denominator of the ratio by 2 to find the rate at which Shelly ran in miles per hour.

$$\frac{2 \text{ miles} \times 2}{0.5 \text{ hour} \times 2} = \frac{\boxed{} \text{ miles}}{1 \text{ hour}}$$

GO ON ⇒

2 A machine can fill 50 bottles per second. Which equation shows this proportional relationship? In the equations, s is the number of seconds and b is the number of bottles.

Ⓐ $b = s + 50$ Ⓒ $b = 50s$

Ⓑ $b = 50 - s$ Ⓓ $b = 50/s$

Remember . . .

An equation in the form $y = mx$ shows a proportional relationship. The letter m represents the unit rate. When you graph a proportional relationship, the unit rate is the slope of the graph.

3 A bicycle rider travels at a constant rate of 6 meters per second. Complete the table of ordered pairs below to graph the proportional relationship.

time in seconds (x)	1	2	3	4	5
distance in meters (y)	6				

Use your table to graph the proportional relationship.

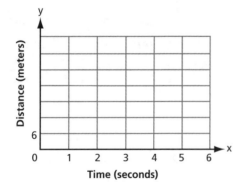

Step-By-Step

Example 2 asks you to find an equation for a proportional relationship.

1 Use the information given in the problem to write the unit rate.

_____ bottles per second

2 The unit rate is the value for m in the general equation $y = mx$. Substitute the unit rate for m.

$y =$ _____x

3 The variables in the problem are b for number of bottles and s for seconds. Substitute those variable for x and y.

$b =$ _____

Step-By-Step

In **example 3**, you use a table to graph a proportional relationship. Tables, graphs, and equations are all possible ways to represent proportional relationships.

1 Use the information in the problem to write an equation.

$y =$ _____

2 Use the equation to complete the table and draw the graph. Connect the points with a straight line.

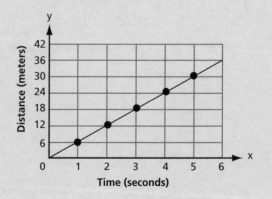

4 Which relationship could be shown by this graph?

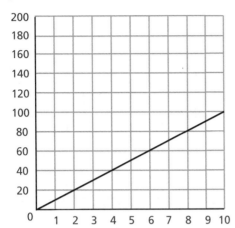

Ⓐ The number of lamps Wesley makes if he makes 10 lamps per week.

Ⓑ The amount Wesley earns if he earns $20 an hour.

Ⓒ The number of birdhouses Wesley builds if he builds one every 4 weeks.

Ⓓ The cost of chairs that are priced at $40 each.

Comparing Proportional Relationships

5 This graph shows a car moving at a constant speed.

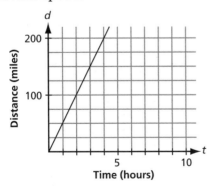

Which equation shows a car moving faster than the car on the graph?

Ⓐ $d = 5t$ Ⓒ $d - t = 55$

Ⓑ $d = 55t$ Ⓓ $d + t = 55$

Step-By-Step

For **example 4**, read the ordered pairs from the graph to decide what the graph shows.

1 Write ordered pairs using 3 or 4 x-values on the graph. Complete the ordered pairs below.

(1, 10)   (3, ☐)

(2, 20)   (4, ☐)

2 Identify the pattern in the ordered pairs.

For every 1-unit increase in the x-value, the y-value increases by—

☐ units.

3 Look for the description of a relationship in which a change of 1 in one value results in a change of 10 in another value.

Step-By-Step

To solve **example 5**, you must compare proportional relationships represented in different ways.

1 Use the general form $y = mx$ to write an equation for the graph. Start by finding m, the unit rate.

$m = $ _____ miles in 1 hour

2 Complete the equation for the graph.

$d = $ _____

3 Look at the answer choices. Find an equation with a greater value of m. This shows a car moving at a greater speed.

GO ON

Try It

Questions 1–2: Complete the table of values for each equation. Then graph the equations on the grids provided.

1 $y = 2x - 3$

x	y
0	−3
1	
2	
3	

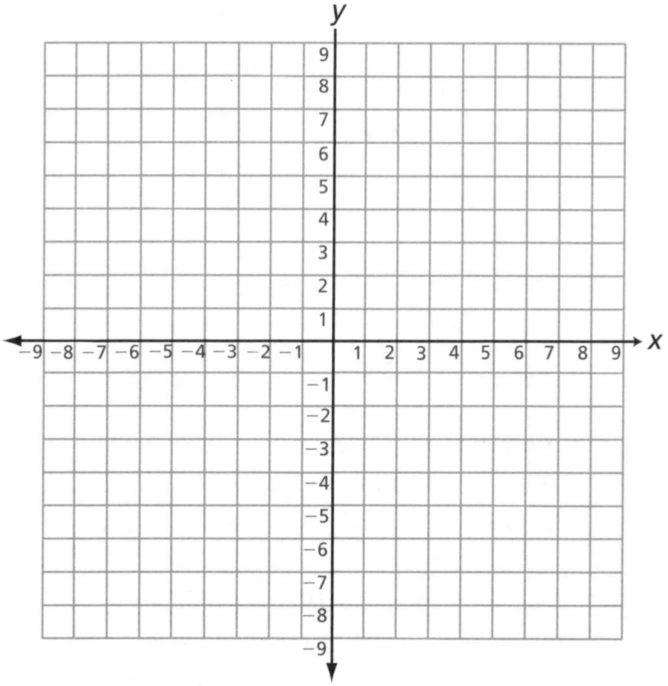

2 $d = -f + 4$

f	d
−2	
−1	
0	4
1	
2	

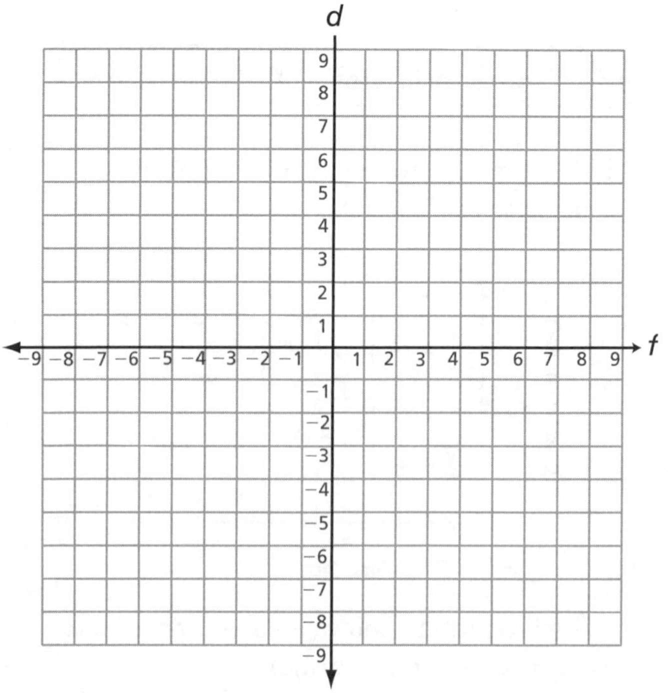

© Perfection Learning® **No reproduction permitted.**

3 Jamal collects eggs from the henhouse every morning. He puts the eggs into cartons and delivers them to local stores to be sold. The stores pay $0.50 per dozen. Jamal uses an equation to determine how much to collect from each store. In the equation shown below, *e* represents the number of eggs Jamal delivers and *C* represents the amount of money he should collect from the store.

$$C = \frac{e}{12} \times \$0.50$$

Use the formula to complete steps **a** through **c** below.

a. Complete the table of values for this equation. Then graph the ordered pairs on the grid to the right. Connect the points and label the line with the equation.

e	C
12	$0.50
24	
60	
84	
144	

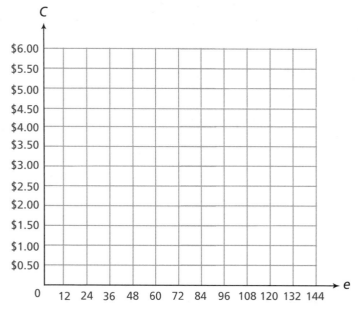

b. Stores pay $0.30 for half-dozen cartons of eggs. Write an equation using *C* to represent the total amount Jamal would collect from sales of half-dozen cartons based on the number of eggs (*e*) he delivers. On the same coordinate grid above, graph and label the equation showing the cost of 6, 18, 60, 72, and 120 eggs sold by the half-dozen.

Equation: _____

c. How much money would the store save by buying 120 eggs in dozen cartons instead of half-dozen cartons?

Answer: _____

GO ON

Slope

6 What is the slope of this line?

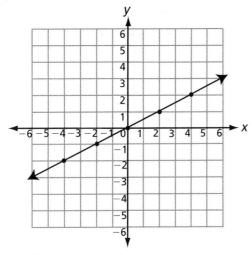

Ⓐ $\frac{1}{2}$ Ⓒ 2

Ⓑ 1   Ⓓ -2

Step-By-Step

To solve **example 6**, you must find the slope of the line that is graphed. Look at the *Slope* box below. Remember that the slope is the ratio of the change in the rise to the change in the run.

1 Find the rise first. The *rise* is the change in value along the y-axis. Subtract the first y-value from the second y-value along the line.

$$y_2 - y_1 = -1 - (-2) = -1 + 2 = 1$$

2 Find the run. The *run* is the change in value along the x-axis. Subtract the first x-value from the second x-value.

$$x_2 - x_1 = -2 - (-4) = -2 + 4 = 2$$

3 Find the slope by writing a ratio for the rise over the run. Simplify the fraction.

Slope

The **slope** m tells you how steep a line is. Slope is a ratio of the change in the y-value (the rise) along a line to the change in the x-value (the run) along the same line. The formula for the finding the slope is—

$$\text{slope} = m = \frac{\text{change in } y\text{-value}}{\text{change in } x\text{-value}} = \frac{y_2 - y_1}{x_2 - x_1}$$

A line with a **positive** slope moves upward from left to right.

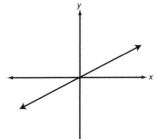

A line with a **negative** slope moves downward from left to right.

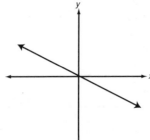

Slope

7 Use this graph.

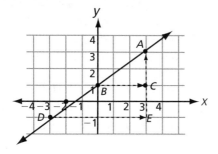

Find the slope using the coordinates of points A and B.

Answer: _____

Find the slope using the coordinates of points A and D.

Answer: _____

Remember . . .

In the graph above, $\triangle ACB$ and $\triangle AED$ are similar right triangles. So, the ratios of the short leg to the long leg must be equal.

Equations for Lines

8 Which equation shows a line that passes through the origin?

Ⓐ $y = x + 1$

Ⓑ $y = x - 1$

Ⓒ $y = 2x$

Ⓓ $y = 2x + 2$

Remember . . .

A line passing through the origin has an equation of the form $y = mx$.

Step-By-Step

In **example 7**, you are asked to compare the slope of a line when you find it in two different ways.

1 Write the ordered pairs for points A and B. Then use them to compute the slope.

$A = (\underline{\quad}, \underline{\quad})$ $B = (\underline{\quad}, \underline{\quad})$

$$m = \frac{3 - 1}{3 - 0} = \frac{\boxed{}}{\boxed{}}$$

2 Use points A and D to compute the slope. Remember to reduce the fraction to simplest form.

$A = (\underline{\quad}, \underline{\quad})$ $D = (\underline{\quad}, \underline{\quad})$

$$m = \frac{3 - (-1)}{3 - (-3)} = \frac{\boxed{}}{\boxed{}} = \frac{\boxed{}}{\boxed{}}$$

Think It Through

To solve **example 8**, remember that the origin has coordinates $(0, 0)$. Find the equation that is true when both x and y are equal to 0.

Choice Ⓐ	$0 = 0 + 1$	false
Choice Ⓑ	$0 = 0 - 1$	false
Choice Ⓒ	$0 = 2 \times 0$	_____
Choice Ⓓ	$0 = (2 \times 0) + 2$	_____

GO ON

9 What is the equation of this line?

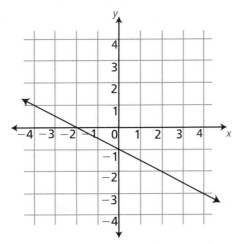

Ⓐ $y = \frac{1}{2}x + 1$ Ⓒ $y = -\frac{1}{2}x + 1$

Ⓑ $y = \frac{1}{2}x - 1$ Ⓓ $y = -\frac{1}{2}x - 1$

Slope-Intercept Form

The slope-intercept form of an equation is

$$y = mx + b$$

where m is slope and b is the y-intercept. The y-intercept is the y-coordinate of the point where a graph crosses the y-axis.

10 What is the y-intercept of the graph of $4x - 3y = 24$?

Ⓐ 6   Ⓒ −6

Ⓑ 8   Ⓓ −8

Remember . . .

To find the y-intercept of an equation, substitute 0 for x and solve for y.

Step-By-Step

Before answering **example 9**, notice that all the answer choices are in slope-intercept form $y = mx + b$. In this form, m is the slope and b is the y-intercept.

1 The line slopes downward from left to right, so it has a negative slope. Which two answer choices does this eliminate?

[ ]   and   [ ]

2 Mark points at (0, −1) and (2, −2). What is the slope of the line?

$$\frac{\text{rise}}{\text{run}} = \frac{-1 - (-2)}{0 - 2} = \frac{1}{-2} = \boxed{}$$

3 What is the y-intercept?

[ ]

4 Use the slope and the y-intercept to write the equation of the line. Then choose the answer choice that matches your equation.

Step-By-Step

Review the definition of the y-intercept in the *Remember* box to answer **example 10**.

1 Substitute 0 for x.

$$4x - 3y = 24$$

$$4(0) - 3y = 24$$

2 Solve for y.

$$0 - 3y = 24$$

$$-3y \div -3 = 24 \div -3$$

$$y = \boxed{}$$

Questions 4–6: Use the graph below.

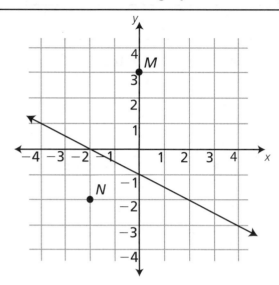

4 What is the slope of the line?

  Ⓐ −2   Ⓒ $-\frac{1}{2}$

  Ⓑ −1   Ⓓ $\frac{1}{2}$

5 What are the x- and y-intercepts?

  x-**intercept:** _____

  y-**intercept:** _____

6 What is the slope of the line through points N and M?

  Ⓐ −2   Ⓒ $-\frac{1}{2}$

  Ⓑ 2   Ⓓ $\frac{5}{2}$

7 What is the slope of the line that passes through the points $(5, -1)$ and $(-3, 2)$?

  Answer: _____

8 What is the slope of the line that passes through the points $(0, 0)$ and $(3, 5)$?

  Ⓐ 0   Ⓒ $\frac{1}{3}$

  Ⓑ $\frac{3}{5}$ Ⓓ $\frac{5}{3}$

9 What is the y-intercept of the graph of $x - 3y = 6$?

  Answer: _____

10 Which equation has a graph that contains the point $(4, 2)$?

  Ⓐ $2x + y = 8$ Ⓒ $x + 2y = 8$

  Ⓑ $2x - y = 8$ Ⓓ $x - 2y = 8$

11 Which is the equation of the line with a slope of -3 that contains the point $(0, 3)$?

  Ⓐ $y = 3 + 3x$ Ⓒ $y = 1 + 3x$

  Ⓑ $y = 3 - 3x$ Ⓓ $y = 1 - 3x$

12 Write an equation in point-slope form for the line with a slope of 1 that contains the point $(2, -6)$.

  Answer: _____

13 Write an equation in slope-intercept form for the line that passes through the points $(-4, 1)$ and $(-1, 4)$.

  Answer: _____

14 Which is the equation of the line that passes through the points $(-2, -4)$ and $(2, -1)$?

  Ⓐ $4x - 3y = 10$ Ⓒ $3x - 4y = 10$

  Ⓑ $4x + 3y = 10$ Ⓓ $3x + 4y = 10$

15 What do the graphs of these equations have in common?

$$y - 4 = 3(x + 1) \qquad y - 4 = -2(x + 1)$$

  Answer: _____

_____

Go for it!

Test Practice 3: Proportional Relationships

Directions: Read and answer each question.

1 Which proportional relationship can be shown with the equation $y = 15x$?

   Ⓐ The amount of money Tasha has left after she spends $15 for a concert ticket

   Ⓑ The amount Tasha spends if she and her sister split a $15 restaurant bill equally

   Ⓒ The amount Tasha earns for 7 hours of babysitting and 8 hours of dog walking

   Ⓓ The amount Tasha earns for babysitting if she charges $15 an hour

2 What is the slope of the line?

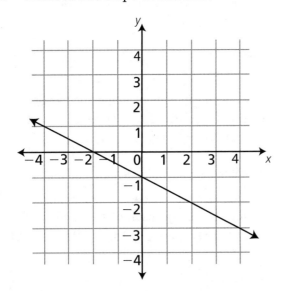

   Ⓐ -2 Ⓒ $-\frac{1}{2}$

   Ⓑ -1 Ⓓ $\frac{1}{2}$

3 What is the y-intercept of the equation $-3x + y = 6$?

   Ⓐ $(0, 3)$ Ⓒ $(0, 6)$

   Ⓑ $(3, 0)$ Ⓓ $(6, 3)$

4 What is the slope of the line?

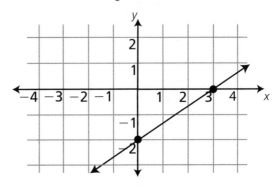

   Ⓐ $\frac{2}{3}$ Ⓒ $-\frac{2}{3}$

   Ⓑ $\frac{3}{2}$ Ⓓ $-\frac{3}{2}$

5 Which is the equation of the line with a slope of -3 that contains the point $(0, 3)$?

   Ⓐ $y = 3 + 3x$ Ⓒ $y = 1 + 3x$

   Ⓑ $y = 3 - 3x$ Ⓓ $y = 1 - 3x$

6 What is the equation of this line?

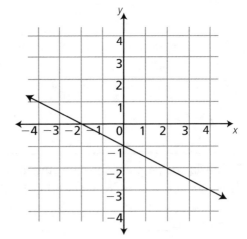

   Ⓐ $y = \frac{1}{2}x + 1$ Ⓒ $y = -\frac{1}{2}x + 1$

   Ⓑ $y = \frac{1}{2}x - 1$ Ⓓ $y = -\frac{1}{2}x - 1$

7 A line has a slope of $\frac{3}{2}$ and a *y*-intercept of -2. What is the equation of the line?

  Ⓐ $y = \frac{3}{2}x - 2$

  Ⓑ $y = -\frac{3}{2}x + 2$

  Ⓒ $y = -2x + \frac{3}{2}$

  Ⓓ $y = \frac{2}{3}x - 2$

8 What is the slope of the line that fits this data?

x	y
−1	−3
0	1
1	5
2	9
3	13

  Ⓐ $\frac{1}{2}$

  Ⓑ 1

  Ⓒ 2

  Ⓓ 4

9 Susan rode her bike 30 kilometers in 2.5 hours. How fast did she ride her bike in kilometers per hour?

  Ⓐ 20 km/hr   Ⓒ 12 km/hr

  Ⓑ 18 km/hr   Ⓓ 10 km/hr

10 What proportional relationship could be represented by this graph?

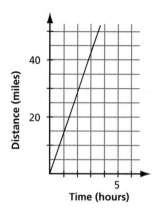

  Ⓐ Mark bicycled for less than 5 hours.

  Ⓑ Mark bicycles 15 mph faster than Marcy.

  Ⓒ Mark bicycles at a speed of 15 miles per hour.

  Ⓓ Mark is bicycling at a steadily increasing speed.

11 Sue Lee made a graph to show what she charges for her dog-walking service. Two points on the graph are (3, 60) and (8, 160). What is the slope of Sue Lee's graph?

  Ⓐ $\frac{1}{20}$

  Ⓑ 3

  Ⓒ 8

  Ⓓ 20

GO ON

12 The equation $d = 30t$ shows boat A moving at a constant speed of 30 miles per hour. Boat B is moving faster than boat A. A student graphs equations for both boats on the same grid. Which of these must be true?

Ⓐ The two graphs have the same slope.

Ⓑ The two graphs have different y-intercepts.

Ⓒ The slope for Boat A is greater than the slope for Boat B.

Ⓓ The slope for Boat B is greater than the slope for Boat A.

13 This table shows a proportional relationship.

time in months (x)	1	2	3	4	5
profit in thousands of dollars (y)	1.2	2.4			

What is the profit for 5 months?

Ⓐ $3.60

Ⓑ $6.00

Ⓒ $4,800

Ⓓ $6,000

14 Janelle graphed the equation $y = 0.25x$. Which of these is NOT true of Janelle's graph?

Ⓐ It has a slope of $\frac{1}{4}$.

Ⓑ It has a y-intercept of 0.25.

Ⓒ It passes through the origin.

Ⓓ It shows a proportional relationship.

15 Where does the graph of $y = -3x + 15$ intersect the vertical axis?

Ⓐ $(-3, 15)$

Ⓑ $(0, 15)$

Ⓒ $(15, 0)$

Ⓓ $(15, -3)$

STOP

Number Correct/Total = _____/15

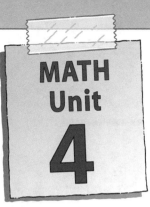

MATH Unit 4

Linear Equations and Systems

Directions: Read and answer each question.

Solving One-Step Equations

1 What is the value of y in this equation?

$$y + 34 = 97$$

Ⓐ 53   Ⓒ 121

Ⓑ 63   Ⓓ 131

Remember . . .

Always perform the same operation on both sides of an equation. Your goal is to isolate the variable on one side of the equal sign.

Step-By-Step

Solve for y in **example 1** by getting it alone on one side of the equation.

1 Undo adding 34 to y by subtracting 34 from each side of the equation.

$$y + 34 = 97$$

$$y + 34 - 34 = 97 - 34$$

2 Simplify the equation to solve for y.

$$y = 97 - 34$$

$$y = \boxed{}$$

Properties of Equations

Property	Definition	Example
Addition Property of Equality	The two sides of an equation will remain equal after you add the *same number* to both sides.	If $a = b$, then $a + c = b + c$.
Subtraction Property of Equality	The two sides of an equation will remain equal after you subtract the *same number* from both sides.	If $a = b$, then $a - c = b - c$.
Multiplication Property of Equality	The two sides of an equation will remain equal after you multiply both sides by the *same number*.	If $a = b$, then $a \times c = b \times c$.
Division Property of Equality	The two sides of an equation will still be equal after you divide both sides by the *same number*.	If $a = b$, then $a \div c = b \div c$.

Solving Two-Step Equations

2 Find the value of *m* in this equation.

$$6m - 24 = 30$$

Ⓐ $m = 1$ Ⓒ $m = 7$

Ⓑ $m = 3$ Ⓓ $m = 9$

Checking an Equation

You can check your solution to an equation by substituting it for the variable.

$$6m - 24 = 30$$

$$6(9) - 24 = 30$$

$$30 = 30$$

3 Solve for *x* when $y = 3x$.

$$5x - y + 8 = x + 12$$

Ⓐ $x = 4$ Ⓒ $x = 2$

Ⓑ $x = 3$ Ⓓ $x = 1$

Remember . . .

To keep an equation balanced, always perform the same operation on both sides of the equation. Use opposite operations.

- To undo addition, subtract.
- To undo subtraction, add.
- To undo multiplication, divide.
- To undo division, multiply.

Step-By-Step

To find the value of *m* in **example 2**, reverse the order of operations to undo the equation.

1 Undo subtracting 24 by adding 24 to each side of the equation.

$$6m - 24 = 30$$

$$6m - 24 + 24 = 30 + 24$$

$$6m = \boxed{}$$

2 Divide both sides of the equation by 6.

$$6m \div 6 = 54 \div 6$$

$$m = \boxed{}$$

Step-By-Step

To answer **example 3**, first substitute $3x$ for *y* and then solve the equation.

1 Substitute $3x$ for *y*.

$$5x - y + 8 = x + 12$$

$$5x - 3x + 8 = x + 12$$

2 Combine like variables.

$$5x - 3x + 8 = x + 12$$

$$\boxed{} + 8 = x + 12$$

3 Solve for *x*.

$$2x + 8 = x + 12$$
$$\underline{ - 8 \qquad - 8}$$
$$2x = x + 4$$
$$\underline{-x = -x}$$

$$x = \boxed{}$$

4 Solve for x.

$$2(x - 5) = x(1 + 6)$$

Ⓐ $x = 2$ Ⓒ $x = \frac{1}{2}$

Ⓑ $x = -2$ Ⓓ $x = -\frac{1}{2}$

The Distributive Property of Multiplication

Addition
For real numbers a, b, and c,

$$a(b + c) = ab + ac$$

$$(b + c)a = ba + ca$$

Subtraction
For real numbers a, b, and c,

$$a(b - c) = ab - ac$$

$$(b - c)a = ba - ca$$

Step-By-Step

Before you can solve **example 4**, you will need to use the distributive property and combine like terms to simplify the equation.

1 Simplify both sides of the equation.

$$2(x - 5) = x(1 + 6)$$

$$2x - 10 = 7x$$

2 Subtract $2x$ from both sides.

$$2x - 10 - 2x = 7x - 2x$$

3 Divide both sides by 5.

$$-10 = 5x$$

$$\boxed{} = x$$

1 Find the value of k in this equation.

$$\frac{k}{3} - 6 = 7$$

Ⓐ $\frac{1}{3}$ Ⓒ $4\frac{1}{3}$

Ⓑ 3 Ⓓ 39

2 Find the value of m in $5m + 7 = 37$.

Ⓐ 6 Ⓒ 150

Ⓑ 8.8 Ⓓ 220

3 Georgia is 12 years old. The sum of her age and her sister's age is 2 less than double Georgia's age.

a. Write an equation to find the age of Georgia's sister. Use s to represent Georgia's sister's age.

Equation: _____

b. Solve the equation. How old is Georgia's sister?

Answer: _____

4 Kyle uses the formula below to convert Celsius temperatures to Fahrenheit. C represents the temperature in Celsius and F represents the temperature in Fahrenheit.

$$F = \frac{9}{5}C + 32$$

Kyle calculated a temperature of 86° F. What temperature is that in Celsius?

Ⓐ $30°$ C   Ⓒ $97°$ C

Ⓑ $65°$ C   Ⓓ $212°$ C

5 Dawn runs on the track at school. She has made a goal of running a certain number of laps in the next 7 days. She's decided that if she runs at least 20 laps a day, she will be able to meet her goal.

a. Write an inequality that you could use to find out how many laps Dawn set as her goal. Use g to represent the number of laps in her goal.

Inequality: _____

b. Solve the inequality. Use the same steps you would if you were solving an equation. What is the most number of laps Dawn could have set as her goal?

Answer: _____

6 Miguel bought 4 packages of hot dogs and 5 packages of hot dog buns for a cookout. The hot dog buns came 6 to a package. Miguel bought at least as many hot dog buns as he bought hot dogs.

a. Write an inequality that you could use to determine the number of hot dogs in each package Miguel bought if there are the same number of hot dogs in each package.

Inequality: _____

b. Solve the inequality. What is the number of hot dogs in each package Miguel purchased?

Answer: _____

5 Which equation has infinitely many solutions?

(A) $5x = 6x$

(B) $8 - x = 12 - (4 + x)$

(C) $x + 3 = x + 8$

(D) $5x + 2 = 2x + 5$

Solutions of Linear Equations

When you simplify a linear equation in one variable, three results are possible.

If $x = a$, there is one solution.

If $a = a$, there are infinitely many solutions.

If $a = b$, there is no solution.

Step-By-Step

To solve **example 5**, simplify the equation in each answer choice.

1 Choice A: Subtract $5x$ from both sides. You get $0 = x$. The solution is 0, so there is one solution.

2 Choice B: Simplify the right side. You get $8 - x = 8 - x$. Add x to both sides and you get $8 = 8$. Any number makes this true. There are infinitely many solutions. The correct answer is B.

3 Check the other two answer choices. For choice C there is no solution. For choice D there is one solution.

Graphing Systems of Equations

6 Graph the following system of equations.

$$y + \frac{3}{2}x - 3 = 0$$

$$y - x + 2 = 0$$

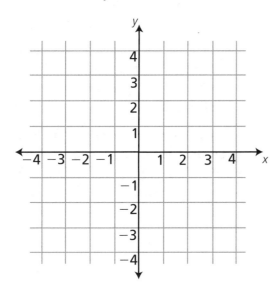

Which point is the solution of the system of equations?

Ⓐ $(-2, 0)$ Ⓒ $(4, 2)$

Ⓑ $(2, 0)$ Ⓓ $(4, -3)$

Step-By-Step

Follow these steps to answer **example 6**.

1 Graph the equations on the same grid. First solve for y, then use the slope-intercept form to graph each equation.

$$y + \frac{3}{2}x - 3 = 0$$

$$y = -\frac{3}{2}x + 3$$

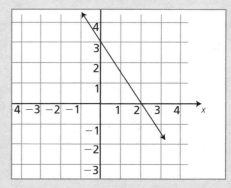

2 The grid above shows the graph of the first equation. Now graph $y - x + 2 = 0$. First solve for y.

$$y - x + 2 = 0$$

$$y = x - 2$$

3 Use the slope of 1 and the y intercept of -2 to graph the second line.

4 The point where the two lines intersect, the **point of intersection**, is the solution to the system.

Systems of Equations

A **system of equations** is two or more related linear equations. The solution set of a system of equations is all the ordered pairs that make both equations true. For example, the solution to the system on the right is the **point of intersection** $(-2, 1)$.

There are several ways to solve systems of equations, including *graphing*, the *substitution method*, and the *elimination method*.

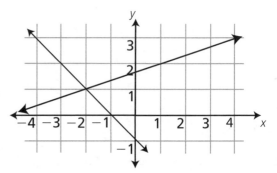

Solving Systems of Equations

7 What is the solution of this system of equations? Solve using substitution.

$$y = 6x - 4$$
$$y = -2x + 28$$

Ⓐ (4, 10)   Ⓒ (10, 8)

Ⓑ (4, 20)   Ⓓ (20, 4)

Real-World Problems and Systems

8 Choose the system of equations that represents the problem situation below.

Lucinda paid $28 for 3 lb of cherries and 2 lb of apples. Her sister paid $17 for 2 lb of cherries and 1 lb of apples. Which system can be solved to find the price per pound of each fruit?

Ⓐ $(2 + 3)a = 28$ Ⓒ $3c + 2a = 28$
   $(2 + 1)c = 17$ $2c + a = 17$

Ⓑ $3(c + a) = 28$ Ⓓ $2c + a = 28$
   $2(c + a) = 17$ $3c + 2a = 17$

Step-By-Step

Use substitution to solve the system of equations in **example 7**.

1 Start with one of the equations.

$$y = 6x - 4$$

2 Substitute $-2x + 28$ for y. Then solve for x.

$$-2x + 28 = 6x - 4$$
$$-2x + 28 + 2x = 6x - 4 + 2x$$
$$28 = 8x - 4$$
$$28 + 4 = 8x - 4 + 4$$
$$32 = 8x$$
$$4 = x$$

3 Solve for the other variable in either equation.

$$y = -2(4) + 28$$
$$y = -8 + 28$$
$$y = 20$$

4 The solution is (____ , ____).

Step-By-Step

The first equation in **example 8** represents what Lucinda spent on cherries and apples. The second equation represents what her sister spent on cherries and apples.

1 Complete this expression for the amount Lucinda spends.

$$3c + \boxed{} \times a$$

2 Complete the equation for Lucinda.

$$3c + 2a = \boxed{}$$

3 Complete the equation for her sister.

$$2c + a = \boxed{}$$

GO ON

7   What is the solution of this system?

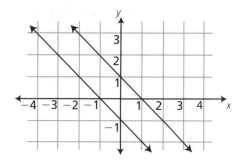

Ⓐ (1, 0)   Ⓒ (−1, 1)

Ⓑ (−1, 0)   Ⓓ {∅}

8   Solve by graphing.

$$y + 4x = 2 \qquad y + 3 = x$$

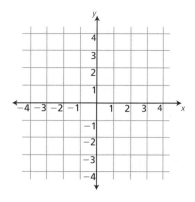

Answer: _____

Questions 9–12: Solve using the substitution method.

9 $y = 4x - 8$

$y = 2x + 10$

Answer: _____

10 $3x - 6y = 30$

$y = -6x + 34$

Ⓐ (6, −2)   Ⓒ (−2, 6)

Ⓑ (3, 1)   Ⓓ (0, 6)

11 $y = 5x + 8$

$y = -10x + 3$

Answer: _____

12 $x - 1.2y = -3$

$0.2y + 0.6x = 12$

Answer: _____

Go for it!

Test Practice 4: Linear Equations and Systems   Estimated time: 25 minutes

Directions: Read and answer each question.

1   Find the value of t in this equation.

$$4t + 6 = 5$$

Ⓐ -4 Ⓒ 2.75

Ⓑ -0.25 Ⓓ 4

2   Which ordered pair is the solution to this system of equations?

$$5x + 2y = 11 \qquad 7x + y = 10$$

Ⓐ $(1, 3)$ Ⓒ $(\frac{1}{2}, \frac{17}{4})$

Ⓑ $(-1, 8)$ Ⓓ $(-1, 17)$

3   If $4x + 3 = -13$, what is the value of x?

Ⓐ 4 Ⓒ 22.5

Ⓑ 2.5 Ⓓ -4

4   Which equation has no solution?

Ⓐ $2x + 1 = 6x + 1$

Ⓑ $2x + 4 = 2x + 10$

Ⓒ $3x + 3 = 6x + 6$

Ⓓ $x + 2 \times 6 = 4 \times 3 + x$

5   Find the value of x in this equation.

$$2x + 4 = 10$$

Answer: _____

6   Solve for x when $y = 2x + 1$.

$$16 + 2y = x + 27$$

Ⓐ $x = 12$ Ⓒ $x = 9$

Ⓑ $x = 10$ Ⓓ $x = 3$

7   Solve by graphing.

$$2x + y = -2$$
$$y = x + 1$$

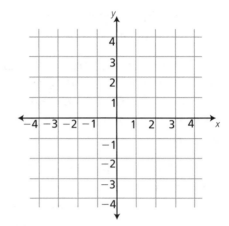

Ⓐ $(-1, 0)$ Ⓒ $(0, -1)$

Ⓑ $(0, -2)$ Ⓓ $(0, 1)$

8   Which equation has exactly one solution?

Ⓐ $4x + 4 = 10$

Ⓑ $4x = 4x + 10$

Ⓒ $4x - 4 = 4x + 4$

Ⓓ $4x + 4x = 8x + 8$

9   What is the solution to this system of equations?

$$y = x - 2$$
$$2x + 2y = 4$$

Ⓐ $(-2, 4)$ Ⓒ $(3, 1)$

Ⓑ $(2, 0)$ Ⓓ $(0, 2)$

GO ON

10 Find the value of f in $3f - 2 = 16$.

Ⓐ $f = 18$
Ⓑ $f = 6$
Ⓒ $f = 4\frac{2}{3}$
Ⓓ $f = 3$

11 Choose the system of equations that represents the problem situation below.

Charlie's Canoe Rental charges $35 per day plus $9 per hour. Lakeside Canoes charges $50 per day plus $6 per hour. Use h for the number of hours and r for the total rental cost.

Ⓐ $r = 6(h + 35)$
$\ r = 9(h + 50)$
Ⓒ $r = 6h + 35$
$\ r = 9h + 50$
Ⓑ $r = 9(h + 35)$
$\ r = 6(h + 50)$
Ⓓ $r = 9h + 35$
$\ r = 6h + 50$

12 Find the value of k in $\frac{k}{7} + 6 = 55$.

Answer: _____

13 Find the value of x in the equation.

$$\frac{x}{3} - 4 = 8$$

Ⓐ $x = 36$
Ⓒ $x = 4$
Ⓑ $x = 12$
Ⓓ $x = 3$

14 What is the solution to this system?

$$5x + y = 20$$

$$x - 2y = 26$$

Ⓐ $(6, 10)$
Ⓒ $(6, -10)$
Ⓑ $(-6, 10)$
Ⓓ $(-6, -10)$

Number Correct/Total = _____ /14

Functions

1 Relations and Functions **[8.F.1]**
2 Tables and Equations for Functions **[8.F.2]**
3 Graphs for Functions **[8.F.2]**
4 Linear and Nonlinear Functions **[8.F.3]**
5 Modeling with Functions **[8.F.4, 8.F.5]**
6 Slope and Rate of Change **[8.F.4]**

Directions: Read and answer each question.

Relations and Functions

1 Which ordered pair is a member of the relation shown in this mapping?

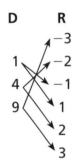

   Ⓐ (9, −3)   Ⓒ (1, 4)
   Ⓑ (1, 3)   Ⓓ (3, 9)

Remember . . .

A **relation** is any set of ordered pairs. The set of first coordinates is called the domain (*D*). The set of second coordinates is the range (*R*).

Step-By-Step

Follow these steps to answer **example 1**.

1 Use the diagram to list all the ordered pairs in the relation.

Domain	Range
1	−1
1	1
4	−2
4	2
9	−3
9	3

2 Find the answer choice that is one of the ordered pairs shown in the table.

Relations and Functions

2 Which set of ordered pairs is a function?

Ⓐ {(1, 2), (1, 3), (1, 4), (1, 5)}

Ⓑ {(1, 2), (2, 4), (3, 6), (4, 8)}

Ⓒ {(1, 5), (3, 0), (2, 1), (3, 2)}

Ⓓ {(2, 3), (3, 3), (3, 2), (2, 2)}

Step-By-Step

1 In **example 2**, choice Ⓐ can be eliminated because 1 is paired with more than one number.

2 What other two choices can be eliminated?

[   ] and [   ]

3 Which graph shows a function?

Ⓐ 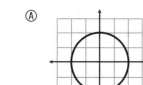   Ⓒ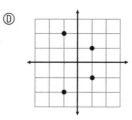

Ⓑ 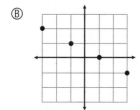   Ⓓ

Step-By-Step

When identifying the graph in **example 3** that represents a function, remember that a function pairs each element of the domain with *exactly* one element of the range. If a vertical line intersects the graph in more than one point, the relation is not a function. This is called the *vertical line test*.

1 Use the vertical line test to show that choice Ⓐ is not a function.

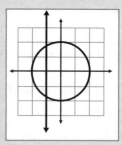

2 Draw vertical lines on choices Ⓑ, Ⓒ, and Ⓓ. Which other two are not functions?

[   ] [   ]
        and

Remember . . .

A **function** is a relation that pairs each element of the domain with exactly one element of the range. In a function, each value of *x* (input) can have only one value for *y* (output).

Tables and Equations for Functions

4 Which rule was used to create this function?

Input	Output
40	20
35	15
30	10
25	5

- Ⓐ Subtract 20.
- Ⓑ Divide by 2.
- Ⓒ Divide by 5.
- Ⓓ Subtract 5.

5 Which rule describes the relationship between the x and y values in this T–Table?

x	y
1	3
2	6
3	9
4	12

- Ⓐ $x + 2 = y$
- Ⓒ $3x = y$
- Ⓑ $x + 4 = y$
- Ⓓ $x \div 3 = y$

Remember . . .

Functions can be described with tables, equations, or graphs.

Step-By-Step

For **example 4**, you have to choose the rule that was applied to the input numbers to create the output numbers.

1 Compare the first pair of input and output numbers, 40 and 20.

You can subtract 20 or divide by 2 to get from 40 to 20.

$$40 - 20 = 20 \text{ and } 40 \div 2 = 20$$

2 Decide if subtracting 20, dividing by 2, or some other operation works for the second pair of numbers, 35 and 15.

$$35 - 20 = 15$$

3 Check to see if the operation that works for the first two pairs of numbers works for the remaining input and output numbers. Then choose the correct rule.

---

1 Look at the first row of numbers in **example 5**. Think: What can I do to 1 to get 3?

I could add 2: $1 + 2 = 3$

2 Try the rule *add 2* to see if it works with the second row of the table.

$$2 + 2 \neq 6$$

3 The rule *add 2* does not work. Try another rule. How about *multiply by 3*?

$$1 \times 3 = 3$$
$$2 \times 3 = 6$$

4 It works! Check to see if the rule works for all rows. Then use the variables x and y to write the rule.

$$\boxed{} \quad x = y$$

GO ON

1 What is the value of this function at $x = 3$?

$$f(x) = 2x + 1$$

- Ⓐ 1
- Ⓒ 7
- Ⓑ 3
- Ⓓ 8

2 A function T doubles each value in the domain. Complete this description of the function.

Answer: $T(x) =$ _____

3 Write this relation as a set of ordered pairs.

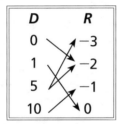

Answer:

4 Which shows the function y that pairs n with $n + 1$?

- Ⓐ $y(n) = y + 1$
- Ⓒ $y(n) = n + 1$
- Ⓑ $y(n) = n$
- Ⓓ $y(n) = n + y$

5 Explain why this table shows a relation but not a function.

5	6
2	4
3	7
2	3

Answer: _____

_____

6 A function R pairs each real number with its reciprocal. Complete this description of the function.

Answer: $R(x) =$ _____

7 Given $g(x) = x^2 - 1$, find $g(5)$.

- Ⓐ 4
- Ⓒ 16
- Ⓑ 9
- Ⓓ 24

8 Let $f(x) = 3x - 1$. What is $f(-1)$?

Answer: _____

6 Which table shows only ordered pairs that belong to the function represented on the graph?

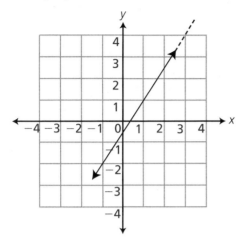

Ⓐ

x	y
1	1
1	2
3	3

Ⓒ

x	y
1	1
−1	−2
3	4

Ⓑ

x	y
0	−1
−1	−2
5	6

Ⓓ

x	y
−2	−1
4	3
1	1

7 In the function shown above, what is the value of y when $x = 3$?

Ⓐ $2\frac{1}{3}$

Ⓑ 3

Ⓒ $3\frac{1}{2}$

Ⓓ 4

Think It Through

To answer **example 6**, check the coordinates in the tables against the graph of the line. When you find a point that is not on the line, rule out that table. Remember, the x-coordinate tells how many units to the left or right of the origin a point is. The y-coordinate tells how many units above or below the origin a point is.

Table Ⓐ: (1, 1) is a point on the line, but (1, 2) is not. ✗

Table Ⓑ: (0, −1) is not a point on the line. ✗

Table Ⓒ: (1, 1) and (−1, −2) are points on the line, and the line would pass through (3, 4). ✔

Think It Through

For **example 7**, extend the line of the graph to find the value of y for $x = 3$.

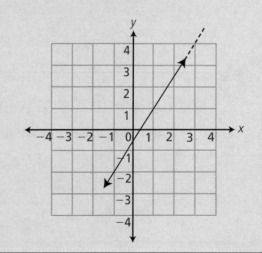

GO ON

Linear and Nonlinear Functions

8 Which is the graph of a nonlinear function?

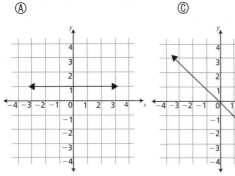

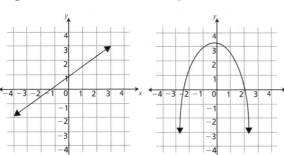

9 Which equation shows a linear relationship?

Ⓐ $3 = xy$ Ⓒ $y = 3x + 1$

Ⓑ $y = \frac{1}{x}$ Ⓓ $y = 4x^2 + 1$

Remember . . .

Linear relationships are expressed in these forms:

$$y = mx + b$$

$$ax + by = c$$

Step-By-Step

In **example 9**, you are to find the equation that shows a linear relationship. You could graph each equation until you found the one that results in a straight line. Here is a quicker solution.

1 Linear equations have two forms:

$$y = mx + b$$

$$ax + by = c$$

2 Look for the answer choice expressed in one of the two forms above.

10   What is the range of the function shown at the right?

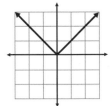

Ⓐ $y > 0$ Ⓒ $y < 0$

Ⓑ $y \geq 0$ Ⓓ $y \leq 0$

Questions 11–12: The domain of this function is the set of all real numbers. Use the function to answer the questions.

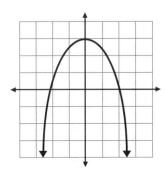

11   What is the maximum value of the function?

Ⓐ $y = -3$ Ⓒ $y = 2$

Ⓑ $y = 3$ Ⓓ $y = 0$

12   What is the range?

Answer: _____

GO ON

13 Which value is excluded from the domain of this function?

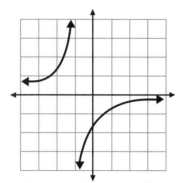

Ⓐ $x = 0$ Ⓒ $x = -1$

Ⓑ $x = 1$ Ⓓ $x = -2$

14 Which graph shows a function?

Ⓐ

Ⓒ
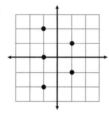

Ⓑ
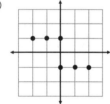

Ⓓ
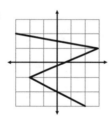

15 Draw a vertical line to show that this set of ordered pairs is not a function.

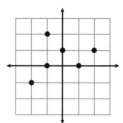

16 What is the domain and range of this relation?

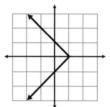

Domain: _____

Range: _____

Modeling with Functions

10 Mr. Taylor made this input/output table for his art budget. He starts with $350 and plans to use $75 per month.

Month	1	2	3	4
Amount Left	$350	$275		

What is the independent variable in this situation?

Ⓐ the number of months

Ⓑ the amount left over

Ⓒ the total starting amount

Ⓓ the amount used per month

11 Mark is packing mugs into cartons. Each carton holds 6 mugs.

Part A Complete the table of ordered pairs.

Cartons (x)	1	2	3	4	5
Mugs (y)	6				

Part B Graph the ordered points and connect them. Remember to complete the y-axis scale.

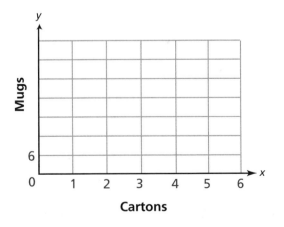

Think It Through

Tables such as the one in **example 10** show the relationship between input values and output values. The output value *depends* on the change in the input value. Therefore, the output value is the **dependent variable** and the input value is the **independent variable**.

To identify the independent variable in **example 10**, then, you must identify the input value.

Step-By-Step

The table in **example 11** shows a relation. A **relation** is a set of ordered pairs in the form (x, y) that are related in some way.

1 Write an equation showing the relationship between the number of mugs (y) and the number of cartons (x).

number of mugs = 6 × number of cartons

$$y = 6x$$

2 Use the equation to complete the table of ordered pairs.

Cartons (x)	1	2	3	4	5
Mugs (y)	6	12	18		

3 Complete the scale of the y-axis. Then graph the ordered pairs on the coordinate grid and connect them.

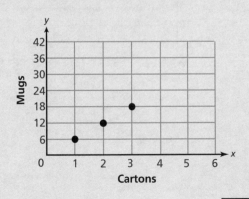

GO ON

Open-Ended Practice

Some tests include questions in which you must explain how you solved a problem. You may also be asked to show your work, draw graphs, or make diagrams. The example below will give you practice responding to such questions.

Modeling with Functions

12 Darren recorded the number of weekly hits his Web site received since the day he first put up the site. He found that the equation $f(x) = 5x^2$ roughly shows the number of hits his site received for each of the first 3 weeks. (The variable x represents the week number.)

Make a graph of the hits for the first three weeks on the coordinate grid below. Then use your graph to estimate the total number of hits his site will receive during week 4.

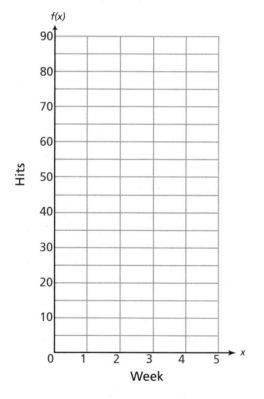

Step-By-Step

To solve **example 12**, first make a plan either mentally or on paper. Then show each step of your plan.

My plan: *I will make a table of ordered pairs. Then I will graph them. I will extend the graph to estimate the number of hits in week 4.*

1 Make a table of ordered pairs for $f(x) = 5x^2$ for the x values 1, 2, and 3.

x	1	2	3
$f(x)$			

2 Graph the ordered pairs on the coordinate grid. Then extend the graph following the trend.

3 The graph shows that the number of hits is about 80 when the value of x is 4. Check your answer by substituting 4 for the value of x in the equation.

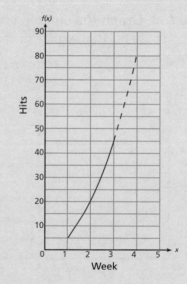

$$f(x) = 5x^2 = 5(4^2) = 5(16) = 80$$

13 A line passes through points $(-2, -3)$ and $(1, -2)$. What is the slope of the line?

Ⓐ -3

Ⓑ $-\frac{1}{3}$

Ⓒ $\frac{1}{3}$

Ⓓ 3

Rate of Change

The **rate of change** of a linear function equals the slope of the line of the graph.

You can use this formula to find the slope of the line that passes through two points (x_1, y_1) and (x_2, y_2).

$$\frac{\text{rise}}{\text{run}} = \frac{y_2 - y_1}{x_2 - x_1}$$

14 An electrician charges \$125 plus \$80 per hour to come to your house and make repairs. This equation represents the cost c in terms of the number of hours h.

$$c = 80h + 125$$

What does the slope of the line represent in the context of the problem situation?

Ⓐ basic charge before the hourly costs are added

Ⓑ costs of materials that are added to the bill

Ⓒ the amount charged per hour

Ⓓ the total amount of the bill

Think It Through

Slope is the steepness of a line. One way to define slope is the ratio of rise over run. Find the difference between the y-coordinates to find the rise of the line in **example 13**. Find the difference between the x-coordinates to find the run.

$$\frac{\text{rise}}{\text{run}} = \frac{y_2 - y_1}{x_2 - x_1} = \frac{-2 - (-3)}{1 - (-2)} = \frac{}{}$$

Step-By-Step

In **example 14**, remember that the slope often represents a rate such as miles per hour.

1 What quantity changes as the number of hours increase?

2 What rate is described in the problem situation?

Go for it!

Test Practice 5: Functions

Estimated time: 20 minutes

Directions: Read and answer each question.

1 Which set of ordered pairs is a function?

Ⓐ {(1.6, 2), (1.4, 1), (1.4, 2)}

Ⓑ {(0.3, 33), (0.2, 22), (0.3, 333)}

Ⓒ {(−2, 4), (−2, 1), (−2, 8)}

Ⓓ {(4, −2), (1, −2), (8, −2)}

2 Which relationship could be shown by this graph?

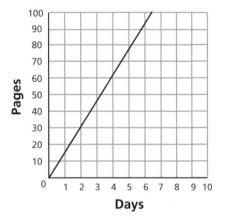

Ⓐ the number of pages Joyce reads if she reads 15 pages each day

Ⓑ the number of days it takes Joyce to read a book if she reads 20 pages a day

Ⓒ the number of books Joyce can read if she reads 5 books a month

Ⓓ the number of weeks it takes Joyce to read a book if she reads 100 pages a week

3 Which table below contains points shown on this graph?

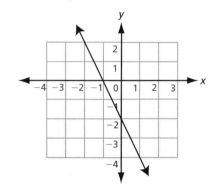

Ⓐ

x	y
−3	3
−2	2
−1	1

Ⓒ

x	y
−1	0
2	0
−2	2

Ⓑ

x	y
−1	0
0	−2
1	−4

Ⓓ

x	y
0	−2
1	−4
2	−2

4 Which rule is true for all of the pairs of values in the table?

x	−2	0	2	4
y	−5	−1	3	7

Ⓐ $y = x − 3$

Ⓑ $y = 3x + 1$

Ⓒ $y = 2x + 1$

Ⓓ $y = 2x − 1$

5 Examine the following table.

x	y
−1	−3
0	1
1	5
2	9
3	13

Which equation shows the relationship between x and y?

Ⓐ $y = 5x − 3$

Ⓑ $y = 2x + 1$

Ⓒ $y = x^2 + 3$

Ⓓ $y = 4x + 1$

6 A function I pairs each real number with its opposite. Which ordered pair belongs to this function?

Ⓐ $(−5, 5)$ Ⓒ $(5, \frac{1}{5})$

Ⓑ $(−5, \frac{1}{5})$ Ⓓ $(\frac{1}{5}, 1)$

7 Which set of numbers completes this function table for the equation below?

$$y = \frac{1}{2}x + 4$$

x	−2	0	4
y			

Ⓐ 3, 4, 6   Ⓒ 0, 4, 6

Ⓑ 5, 4, 8   Ⓓ −3, 0, 4

8 What rule is shown in this table?

x	15	30	5	25
y	3	6	1	5

Ⓐ $y = x − 12$

Ⓑ $y = x − 20$

Ⓒ $y = 5x$

Ⓓ $y = \frac{x}{5}$

9 Which graph shows a function?

Ⓐ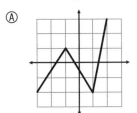

Ⓒ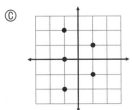

Ⓑ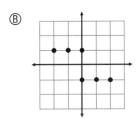

Ⓓ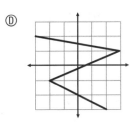

10 Which rule describes the pattern in this chart?

A	B
1	6
2	11
3	16
4	21

Ⓐ $5A + 1 = B$ Ⓒ $6A = B$

Ⓑ $6A − 3 = B$ Ⓓ $A + 5 = B$

GO ON

11 Which table gives the ordered pairs for the graph of a nonlinear equation?

Ⓐ
x	y
−3	3
−2	1
2	1
3	3

Ⓒ
x	y
1	5
2	6
3	7
4	8

Ⓑ
x	y
−3	1
−5	2
−7	3
−9	4

Ⓓ
x	y
4	8
6	12
8	16
10	20

12 Which ordered pair belongs to this function?

$$P(x) = 2x^2 + 5$$

Ⓐ (3, 11)   Ⓒ (3, 17)
Ⓑ (11, 3)   Ⓓ (3, 23)

13 Which set of ordered pairs is a function?

Ⓐ {(−1, 2), (0, −1), (1, 2), (0, 0)}
Ⓑ {(−1, 3), (0, 0), (−1, 4), (2, 0)}
Ⓒ {(−1, 10), (0, 8), (1, 6), (2, 4)}
Ⓓ {(−1, 6), (0, 2), (−1, 4), (2, 6)}

14 Which ordered pair is a member of the relation shown in this mapping?

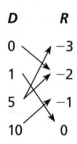

Ⓐ (−3, 0)   Ⓒ (1, −1)
Ⓑ (0, −2)   Ⓓ (−3, 5)

15 Which number correctly completes this table?

x	−2	−1	0	1	2
y	4	2	0		−4

Ⓐ 2   Ⓒ −1
Ⓑ 1   Ⓓ −2

16 Which equation shows a linear relationship?

Ⓐ $x \div y = 8$
Ⓑ $x + y = 8$
Ⓒ $x^2 - y^2 = 8$
Ⓓ $x^2 + y^2 = 8$

17 Which graph does NOT show a function?

Ⓐ 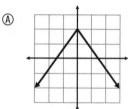   Ⓒ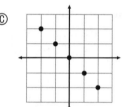

Ⓑ 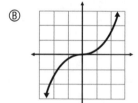   Ⓓ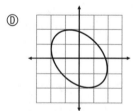

18 Which equation shows the relationship between x and y?

x	y
−1	−2
0	2
1	6
2	10
3	14

Ⓐ $y = 4x$

Ⓑ $y = 4x - 2$

Ⓒ $y = 4x + 2$

Ⓓ $y = x + 4$

19 Which rule was used to make this table?

Input	Output
400	200
300	150
200	100
150	75
100	50

Ⓐ Divide by 2.

Ⓑ Subtract 200.

Ⓒ Subtract 150.

Ⓓ Divide by 3.

20 Which is the graph of a nonlinear function?

Ⓐ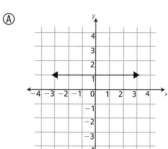

Ⓑ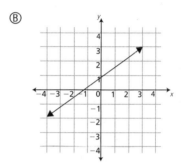

Ⓒ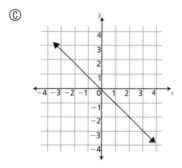

Ⓓ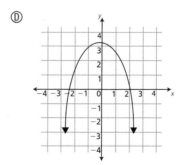

Number Correct/Total = _____ /20

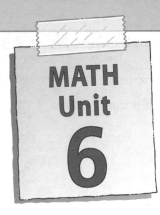

MATH Unit 6

Geometry

1 Translations [**8.G.1, 8.G.3**]
2 Reflections [**8.G.1, 8.G.3**]
3 Rotations [**8.G.1, 8.G.3**]
4 Dilations [**8.G.3**]
5 Congruence and Similarity [**8.G.2, 8.G.4**]
6 Properties of Angles in Triangles [**8.G.5**]
7 Parallel Lines and Transversals [**8.G.5**]
8 Properties of Similar Triangles [**8.G.5**]

Directions: Read and answer each question.

Translations

1 Which describes the movement from A to A' ?

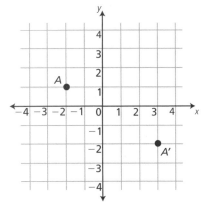

- Ⓐ $(x, y) \rightarrow (x + 5, y - 3)$
- Ⓑ $(x, y) \rightarrow (x - 3, y - 5)$
- Ⓒ $(x, y) \rightarrow (x + 5, y + 3)$
- Ⓓ $(x, y) \rightarrow (x + 3, y - 2)$

Translations

In a **translation**, a figure moves in a straight line. The figure can move left or right, up or down, or in a combination of those directions.

Step-By-Step

In **example 1**, the movement from A to A' is described by the change in the values of the x- and y-coordinates.

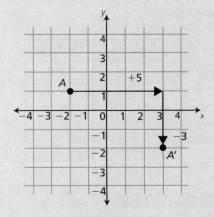

1 Find the change in the x- and y-values between A and A'.

2 Choose the answer that describes increasing the x-value by 5 and decreasing the y-value by 3.

Reflections

2 Suppose the trapezoid shown below is reflected over the *x*-axis. What are the coordinates of the vertices of the reflected figure?

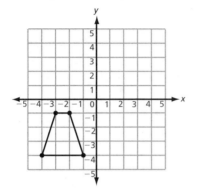

Ⓐ (−2, 1), (−3, 1), (−4, 4), (−1, 4)

Ⓑ (−3, 1), (3, −1), (−4, 4), (−1, 4)

Ⓒ (2, −1), (−3, 1), (−4, 4), (1, −4)

Ⓓ (−2, −1), (−3, 1), (−4, 4), (−1, −4)

Reflections

When a point (*x*, *y*) is reflected across the *x*-axis, the new point is located at (*x*, −*y*).

When a point (*x*, *y*) is reflected across the *y*-axis, the new point is located at (−*x*, *y*).

Think It Through

In **example 2**, the *x*-axis acts like a mirror. The trapezoid will appear to be flipped upward. Each point is the same distance from the *x*-axis in the reflection as it was in the original shape.

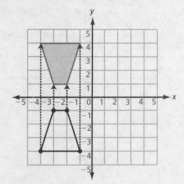

For each reflected point, the *x*-value is the same as the original *x*-value; the *y*-value is the opposite of the original *y*-value.

$$(-2, -1) \rightarrow (-2, 1)$$

$$(-3, -1) \rightarrow (-3, 1)$$

$$(-4, -4) \rightarrow (-4, 4)$$

$$(-1, -4) \rightarrow (-1, 4)$$

Properties of Translations, Reflections, and Rotations

Translations, reflections, and rotations can change the position and orientation of a figure. But, the size and shape do not change. Here are three properties of these transformations.

• Lines are taken to lines, and line segments to line segments of the same length.

• Angles are taken to angles of the same measure.

• Parallel lines are taken to parallel lines.

GO ON

3 If the triangle shown below is rotated 90° clockwise about the origin, what will be the new location of point *A*?

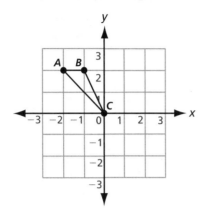

Ⓐ (−2, −2)   Ⓒ (2, 2)

Ⓑ (−1, −2)   Ⓓ (1, 2)

Step-By-Step

In **example 3**, point *C* will stay at the origin, but the other two points will rotate 90° clockwise.

1 Rotate the triangle a quarter of a turn clockwise.

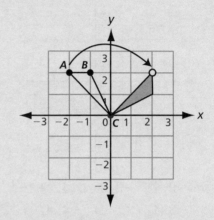

2 Find the coordinates of the new location of point *A*.

(2, ☐)

90° Rotation

If point (*x*, *y*) is rotated 90° clockwise, the new point is located at (*y*, −*x*).

$$(x, y) \rightarrow (y, -x)$$

$$(-1, 2) \rightarrow (2, 1)$$

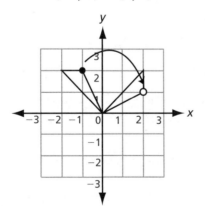

If point (*x*, *y*) is rotated 90° counterclockwise, the new point is located at (−*y*, *x*).

$$(x, y) \rightarrow (-y, x)$$

$$(-1, 2) \rightarrow (-2, -1)$$

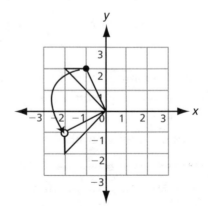

4 The rectangle below is enlarged by a scale factor of 2. The origin is the center of dilation. Which answer gives the coordinates of the dilated image?

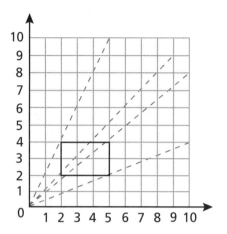

Ⓐ (4, 4), (4, 8), (10, 4), (10, 8)
Ⓑ (4, 4), (4, 8), (4, 10), (4, 8)
Ⓒ (4, 4), (4, 8), (8, 4), (10, 4)
Ⓓ (4, 4), (4, 8), (5, 4), (5, 8)

5 What rule was used to transform *ABC* to *A'B'C'*?

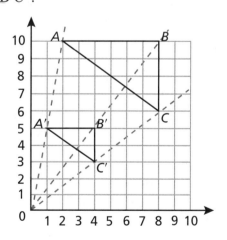

Ⓐ $(x, y) \rightarrow (6x, 6y)$
Ⓑ $(x, y) \rightarrow (3x, 3y)$
Ⓒ $(x, y) \rightarrow (2x, 2y)$
Ⓓ $(x, y) \rightarrow (\frac{1}{2}x, \frac{1}{2}y)$

Think It Through

For **example 4**, multiply the coordinates of the original image by the scale factor.

Multiply the *x*- and *y*-coordinates of each vertex of the rectangle by 2.

$$(2, 2) \rightarrow (2 \times 2, 2 \times 2) = (4, 4)$$

$$(2, 4) \rightarrow (2 \times 2, 2 \times 4) = (4, 8)$$

$$(5, 2) \rightarrow (5 \times 2, 2 \times 2) = (\boxed{}, \boxed{})$$

$$(5, 4) \rightarrow (5 \times 2, 4 \times 2) = (\boxed{}, \boxed{})$$

Dilations

A dilation is a transformation in which a figure is enlarged or reduced by a scale factor. For a dilation in the coordinate plane with the origin as its center, the dilated image of (x, y) is (kx, ky), where k is the scale factor.

Step-By-Step

Write a dilation rule $(x, y) \rightarrow (kx, ky)$ to answer **example 5**.

1 Write the ratio of corresponding side lengths of the image to the preimage.

$$A'B' : AB = 3 : 6 = 1 : 2 = \frac{1}{2}$$

2 Use $\frac{1}{2}$ as the scale factor. Write a rule showing the relationship between the coordinates of the preimage and the coordinates of the image.

$$(x, y) \rightarrow (\boxed{} x, \boxed{} y)$$

3 Check the rule by substituting coordinates for points *A*, *B*, and *C* into the rule and testing to see that it gives the coordinates for *A'*, *B'*, and *C'*.

Questions 1–4: Use this graph to answer the questions.

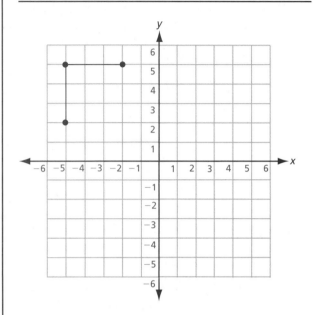

Questions 5–7: Use this graph to answer the questions.

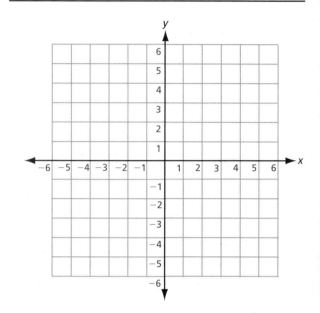

1 Joan needs to plot one more point to complete the square. Which ordered pair describes this point?

Ⓐ $(-2, 2)$ Ⓒ $(-5, 0)$

Ⓑ $(-2, 0)$ Ⓓ $(2, 5)$

2 Find the area of the square.

Ⓐ 3 units^2 Ⓒ 12 units^2

Ⓑ 9 units^2 Ⓓ 18 units^2

3 Translate the square by moving it 6 units to the right and 4 units down.

4 Draw a reflection of the square you drew in question 3. Reflect the shape over the *y*-axis.

5 Plot the points below and connect the points to form a triangle. Which shows the length of an altitude of the triangle?

$$(2, 4), (2, -3), (-4, -3)$$

Ⓐ 1 unit   Ⓒ 5 units

Ⓑ 4 units   Ⓓ 7 units

6 Find the area of the triangle you drew in question 5.

Ⓐ 3 units^2 Ⓒ 21 units^2

Ⓑ 9 units^2 Ⓓ 42 units^2

7 If you translate the triangle 3 units up and 5 units to the left, will the area of the triangle change? Explain your answer.

Answer: _____

_____

_____

8 You want to translate a point up and to the left. What is the procedure for doing that?

Ⓐ Add a positive number to its *x*-coordinate and a positive number to the *y*.

Ⓑ Add a positive number to its *x*-coordinate and a negative number to the *y*.

Ⓒ Add a negative number to its *x*-coordinate and a positive number to the *y*.

Ⓓ Add a negative number to its *x*-coordinate and a negative number to the *y*.

9 In ΔABC, vertex A moves up 2 and right 3. Vertex B moves up 2 and right 3. How must vertex C move if the end result is a simple translation?

Answer: _____

Congruence and Similarity

6 These two triangles are congruent.

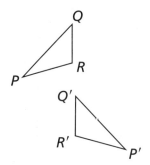

Which sequence of two transformations changes ΔPQR into ΔP'Q'R' ?

Ⓐ flip vertically, then rotate

Ⓑ flip horizontally, then rotate

Ⓒ flip vertically, then translate

Ⓓ flip horizontally, then translate

Step-By-Step

For **example 6**, choose the two transformations that will change one triangle into another. Remember that "flip" is another name for a reflection.

1 Compare the two triangles. They show a reflection and a translation, but not a _____. You can therefore eliminate answer choices _____ and _____.

2 Compare answer choices *C* and *D*. Do the triangles show a vertical or a horizontal flip?

_____

7   These two triangles are similar.

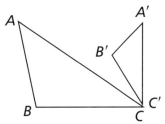

Which sequence of two transformations changes $\triangle ABC$ into $\triangle A'B'C'$?

Ⓐ dilation, then rotation

Ⓑ rotation, then reflection

Ⓒ translation, then rotation

Ⓓ dilation, then translation

Step-By-Step

For **example 7**, choose the two transformations that will change one triangle into another.

1 The triangles are not the same size, so the answer must include a dilation. You can therefore eliminate answer choices _____ and _____.

2 Compare answer choices *A* and *D*. Do the triangles show a rotation or a translation?

_____

Transformations, Congruence, and Similarity

- A two-dimensional figure is congruent to another if the second can be obtained from the first by a sequence of rotations, reflections, and translations.

- A two-dimensional figure is similar to another if the second can be obtained from the first by a sequence of rotations, reflections, translations, and dilations.

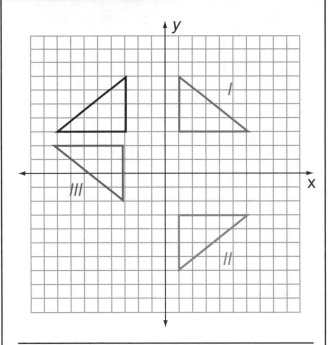

Use the figures above to answer question 10.

10 Which of the figures can be obtained from the original figure through a single translation?

Ⓐ I

Ⓒ III

Ⓑ II

Ⓓ none of them

11 The point (4, 10) is the upper vertex of a triangle. The triangle is reflected about the *y*-axis, dilated by a factor of 2, and then translated up 5. What are the final coordinates of this vertex?

Answer: _____

12 The point (−2, −4) is the lower left vertex of a rectangle. The rectangle is dilated by a factor or 0.5, reflected about the *x*-axis, and then translated left by 3. What is the point's final location?

Use the graph below to help you answer the problem.

Answer: _____

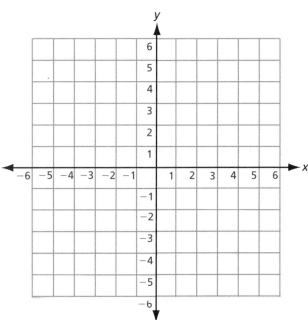

GO ON

Properties of Angles in Triangles

8 What is the measure of ∠*K*?

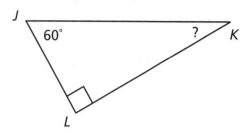

    Ⓐ 30°

    Ⓑ 60°

    Ⓒ 90°

    Ⓓ 120°

Step-By-Step

For **example 8**, use the fact that the sum of the angles must be 180°.

1 Remember that the small square at angle *L* means this is a right angle. What is the measure of ∠*L*?

    ☐ degrees

2 Add the measures of angles *J* and *L*.

    ☐ + 60° = ☐

3 Subtract the sum from 180°.

    180° − ☐ = ☐

9 What is the measure of ∠*E*?

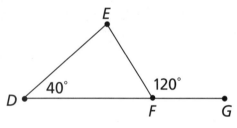

Answer: _____

The Exterior Angle Theorem

An exterior angle of a triangle is equal to the sum of the two remote interior angles.

Step-By-Step

You can solve **example 9** by applying the exterior angle theorem.

1 Use the theorem and the given information to write an equation.

$$m\angle EFG = m\angle D + m\angle E$$

$$120° = \text{_____} + m\angle E$$

2 Solve the equation to find the measure of ∠*E*. Subtract 40° from both sides.

$$120° − 40° = \text{_____}$$

$$\text{_____} = m\angle E$$

Parallel Lines and Transversals

In the figure below, transversal *t* intersects two parallel lines. Use the drawing to answer examples 10 and 11.

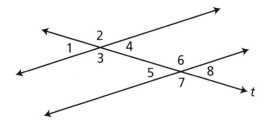

10 Which angle forms a pair of alternate interior angles with ∠4?

   Ⓐ ∠1   Ⓒ ∠5

   Ⓑ ∠2   Ⓓ ∠8

11 Which term describes any pair of corresponding angles in the figure above?

   Ⓐ adjacent   Ⓒ supplementary

   Ⓑ congruent   Ⓓ obtuse

Remember . . .

When a line intersects a pair of parallel lines, 8 angles are formed.

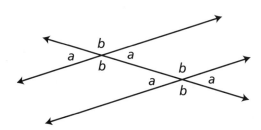

In the figure above—

   Angles labeled *a* are congruent.

   Angles labeled *b* are congruent.

   m∠*a* + m∠*b* = 180°.

Step-By-Step

Follow these steps to solve **example 10**.

1 Identify the interior angles. They are between the two parallel lines.

   interior angles: ∠3, ∠4, ∠5, and ▢

2 Alternate angles fall on opposite sides of the transversal. For example, ∠3 and ∠6 are alternate angles. Which interior angle forms an alternate pair with ∠4?

     ∠4 and ▢

Step-By-Step

Example 11 asks about corresponding angles. Corresponding angles are in the same position from one line to the next. For example, ∠1 and ∠5 are corresponding angles.

1 Study the *Remember* box to the left. Find two corresponding angles in the figure.

2 Any two angles in the figure are either congruent or supplementary. Which term describes the corresponding angles?

   ▢

GO ON

13 What is the measure of ∠C?

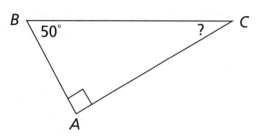

Answer: _____

Use the diagram to answer questions 14 and 15.

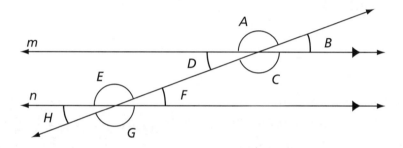

14 Angle C corresponds to which angle?

Answer: _____

15 If m∠C = 140, then what is the m∠D?

Answer: _____

---

16 What is the measure of the interior ∠X?

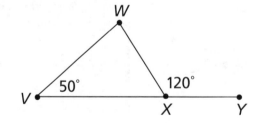

Answer: _____

Properties of Similar Triangles

In the triangles below, $\angle A \cong \angle X$ and $\angle B \cong \angle Y$.

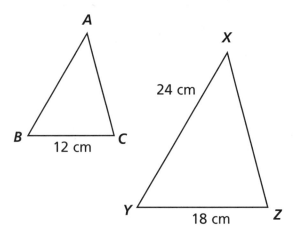

12 Which side completes the proportion?

$$\frac{AB}{XY} = \frac{?}{YZ}$$

Ⓐ AB Ⓒ AC

Ⓑ BC Ⓓ XZ

Step-By-Step

In **example 12**, the two triangles are similar because of the angle-angle condition. Remember that corresponding sides of similar polygons are proportional. A proportion shows that two ratios are equal.

1 It may help you to say the proportion out loud like this—

   AB is to XY as [   ] is to YZ.

2 Notice that the bottom elements of the ratios belong to triangle XYZ. This means that the top elements belong to triangle ABC.

3 Ask yourself: Which side of triangle ABC corresponds to side YZ?

Remember . . .

If two pairs of corresponding angles are congruent, then two triangles must be similar. This is the **angle-angle** condition for proving two triangles are similar.

Similar Figures

Similar figures have corresponding angles that are equal and corresponding sides that have equal ratios. The symbol $\sim$ means *is similar* to.

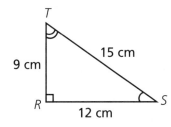

$\triangle RST \sim \triangle WXY$

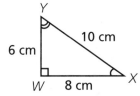

$\angle T = \angle Y$

$\angle R = \angle W$

$\angle S = \angle X$

$\dfrac{RT}{WY} = \dfrac{9}{6} = \dfrac{3}{2}$

$\dfrac{TS}{YX} = \dfrac{15}{10} = \dfrac{3}{2}$

$\dfrac{RS}{WX} = \dfrac{12}{8} = \dfrac{3}{2}$

Go for it!

Test Practice 6: Geometry

Estimated time: 30 minutes

Directions: Read and answer each question.

1 What is the measure of ∠D?

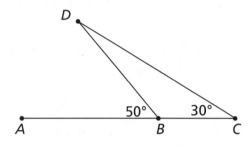

Answer: _____

2 Which sequence of two transformations changes the left triangle into the right triangle?

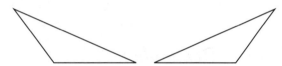

   Ⓐ translate left, reflect across vertical line

   Ⓑ translate right, reflect across vertical line

   Ⓒ translate left, reflect across horizontal line

   Ⓓ translate right, reflect across horizontal line

3 △ABC is dilated by a scale factor of 2 and then rotated 90° clockwise. The result is labeled △DEF. Triangles ABC and DEF must be —

   Ⓐ obtuse.

   Ⓑ similar.

   Ⓒ congruent.

   Ⓓ equilateral.

4 A parallelogram PQRS is rotated 90° counterclockwise. The result is labeled P'Q'R'S'. The sides P'Q' and R'S' must be —

   Ⓐ parallel.

   Ⓑ adjacent.

   Ⓒ not congruent.

   Ⓓ perpendicular.

5 Triangles ABC and XYZ are similar. The measure of ∠A is 50°. Which of the following must be true?

   Ⓐ One triangle is equilateral.

   Ⓑ Both triangles are right triangles.

   Ⓒ One angle in △XYZ measures 50°.

   Ⓓ One angle in △XYZ measures 130°.

Use this figure to answer questions 6 and 7.

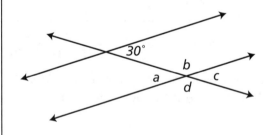

6 Which angle corresponds to the 30° angle?

   Ⓐ ∠a   Ⓒ ∠c

   Ⓑ ∠b   Ⓓ ∠d

7 What is m∠a?

   Ⓐ 15°   Ⓒ 60°

   Ⓑ 30°   Ⓓ 150°

8 If the trapezoid is rotated 90° counterclockwise about the origin, what will be the new location of point *M*?

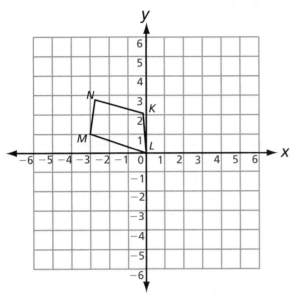

Ⓐ (1, 3)　　Ⓒ (−3, −1)

Ⓑ (−1, −3)　　Ⓓ (3, 1)

9 Which of the following best describes the movement of Figure 1 to Figure 2?

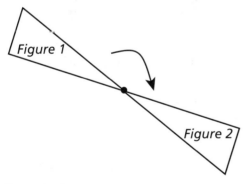

Ⓐ reflection

Ⓑ turn, 90° clockwise

Ⓒ translation

Ⓓ turn, 180° clockwise

10 Line segment *AB* has endpoints at *A*(2, −6) and *B*(8, −6). If $\overline{AB}$ is reflected over the *x*-axis and then translated 4 units to the left to get *A'B'*, what are the endpoints of *A'B'*?

Ⓐ *A'*(2, 6); *B'*(8, 6)

Ⓑ *A'*(−2, −6); *B'*(4, −6)

Ⓒ *A'*(−2, 6); *B'*(4, 6)

Ⓓ *A'*(−6, −6); *B'*(−12, −6)

11 Translate the rectangle 5 units right and 2 units up. What are the coordinates of the translated figure?

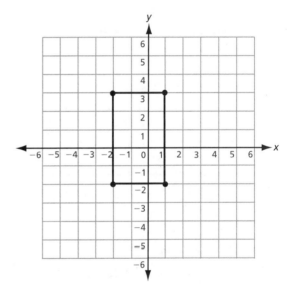

Ⓐ (6, 5), (3, 5), (3, 0), (6, 0)

Ⓑ (6, 1), (3, 1), (3, −4), (1, −4)

Ⓒ (3, 5), (0, 5), (0, 0), (−1, 0)

Ⓓ (2, 1), (5, 1), (5, −4), (2, −4)

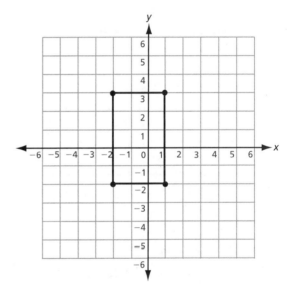

GO ON

12 What is the smallest turn that will rotate this figure onto itself?

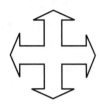

Ⓐ 180° ($\frac{1}{2}$ turn)

Ⓑ 120° ($\frac{1}{3}$ turn)

Ⓒ 90° ($\frac{1}{4}$ turn)

Ⓓ 45° ($\frac{1}{8}$ turn)

13 What transformation is shown in this figure?

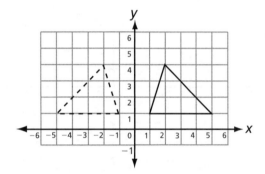

Ⓐ 180° rotation

Ⓑ translation 6 units to the left

Ⓒ reflection across the *x*-axis

Ⓓ reflection across the *y*-axis

14 The shaded arrow is the result of a sequence of transformations of the white arrow. Which of the following is a possible sequence of transformations?

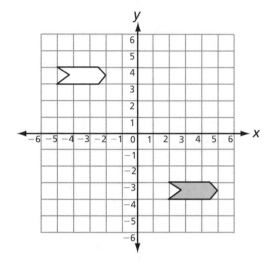

Ⓐ a reflection across the *y*-axis and then a reflection across the *x*-axis

Ⓑ a reflection across the *x*-axis and then a translation 7 units right

Ⓒ a translation 5 units right and 7 units down

Ⓓ a reflection across the *y*-axis and a translation 7 units down

15 What is the measure of angle *R*?

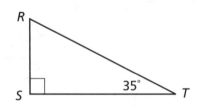

Ⓐ 35°   Ⓒ 65°

Ⓑ 55°   Ⓓ 145°

16 Two angles of a triangle measure 24° and 76°. What is the measure of the third angle?

Ⓐ 280°   Ⓒ 100°

Ⓑ 140°   Ⓓ 80°

17 △*MOP* is similar to △*DOG*. What is the distance between points *O* and *M*?

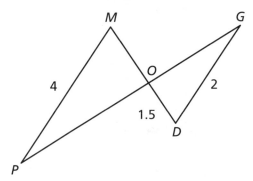

Ⓐ 0.75   Ⓒ 4

Ⓑ 3   Ⓓ 8

In the figure below, lines *a*, *b*, and *c* are parallel. Lines *m* and *n* are transversals. Use the figure to answer questions 18–20.

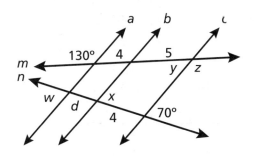

18 Which angle measures 50°?

Ⓐ ∠*w*   Ⓒ ∠*y*

Ⓑ ∠*x*   Ⓓ ∠*z*

19 Which term describes the relationship between ∠*w* and ∠*x*?

Ⓐ alternate interior

Ⓑ alternate exterior

Ⓒ corresponding

Ⓓ congruent

20 What is the measure of ∠*w*?

Ⓐ 50°   Ⓒ 110°

Ⓑ 70°   Ⓓ 130°

---

21 A triangle in the coordinate plane has vertices (−4, 1), (3, 1), and (1, 5). If the triangle is dilated by a scale factor of 2, which answer gives the vertices of the image? The origin is used as the center of the dilation.

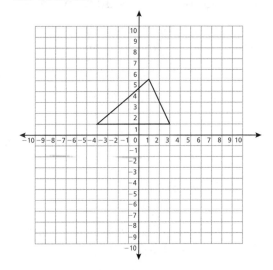

Ⓐ (−8, 2), (6, 2), (2, 10)

Ⓑ (−8, −2), (−6, −2), (−2, −10)

Ⓒ (−4, −2), (6, 1), (2, 5)

Ⓓ (8, 2), (6, 2), (2, 10)

GO ON ▷

Use this figure to answer questions 22 and 23.

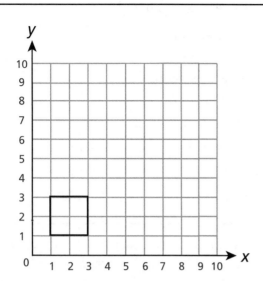

22 What are the coordinates of a dilation of the square using a factor of 3 and the origin as the center of dilation?

Ⓐ (3, 3), (9, 3), (9, 9), (3, 9)

Ⓑ (4, 4), (7, 4), (7, 7), (4, 7)

Ⓒ (3, 3), (6, 6), (6, 9), (9, 3)

Ⓓ (1, 1), (3, 1), (3, 3), (1, 3)

23 What is the motion rule for the dilation in question 22?

Ⓐ $(x, y) \rightarrow (3x, 3y)$

Ⓑ $(x, y) \rightarrow (\frac{1}{3}x, \frac{1}{3}y)$

Ⓒ $(x, y) \rightarrow (x + 3, y + 3)$

Ⓓ $(x, y) \rightarrow (x - 3, y + 3)$

24 If the triangle below is rotated 180° clockwise about the origin, which figure shows the location of the rotated figure?

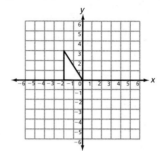

Ⓐ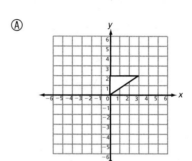

Ⓑ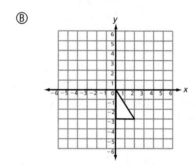

Ⓒ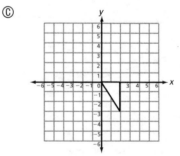

Ⓓ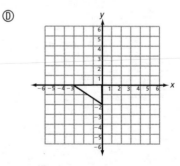

90

Open-Ended Practice

Some tests include questions in which you must explain how you solved a problem. You may also be asked to show your work, draw graphs, or make diagrams. The example below will give you practice responding to such questions.

25 On the coordinate grid below, $\triangle ABC$ was reflected across the x-axis to get the image $\triangle A'B'C'$. Then $\triangle A'B'C'$ was translated left 8 units to get the image $\triangle A''B''C''$.

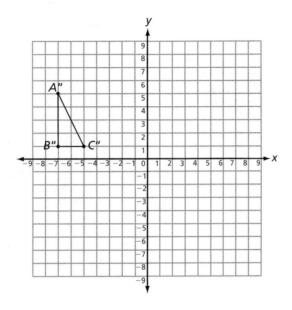

Draw and label $\triangle A'B'C'$ and $\triangle ABC$ on the coordinate grid above.

What are the coordinates of the vertices of $\triangle ABC$?

     vertex A: _____

     vertex B: _____

     vertex C: _____

Number Correct/Total = _____/25

MATH Unit 7

The Pythagorean Theorem and Volume

1 The Pythagorean Theorem **[8.G.7]**
2 Proving the Pythagorean Theorem **[8.G.6]**
3 Applying the Pythagorean Theorem **[8.G.7]**
4 Distance and the Pythagorean Theorem **[8.G.8]**
5 Volumes of Cones, Cylinders, and Spheres **[8.G.9]**

Directions: Read and answer each question.

The Pythagorean Theorem

1 What is the value of c in the right triangle below?

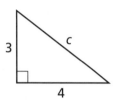

Ⓐ 5   Ⓒ 25
Ⓑ 7   Ⓓ 49

Pythagorean Theorem

The **Pythagorean Theorem** states that $a^2 + b^2 = c^2$ for any right triangle, where a and b are the lengths of the legs and c is the length of the hypotenuse.

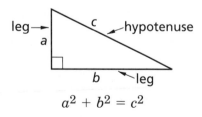

$$a^2 + b^2 = c^2$$

Step-By-Step

In **example 1**, you know the lengths of two sides of a right triangle. You can use the **Pythagorean Theorem** to find the length of the third side. (See the box to the left for a review of the Pythagorean Theorem.)

1 Identify the values that you know. Use a to represent the length of the shortest leg.

$$a = \boxed{}$$

$$b = \boxed{}$$

2 Use the Pythagorean Theorem to write an equation to find the value of c.

$$a^2 + b^2 = c^2$$

$$\boxed{} + \boxed{} = c^2$$

3 Solve for c.

$$3^2 + 4^2 = c^2$$
$$9 + 16 = c^2$$
$$25 = c^2$$
$$\sqrt{25} = c$$
$$\boxed{} = c$$

Proving the Pythagorean Theorem

2 This diagram shows that the Pythagorean Theorem is true for a triangle with sides of 3, 4, and 5.

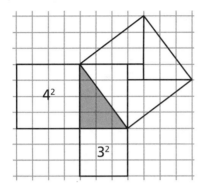

Which expression shows that the square on the hypotenuse has an area of 5^2?

Ⓐ $(4 \times 6) + 1$

Ⓑ $(4 \times 12) + 1$

Ⓒ $\frac{1}{2}(3 \times 4) + 1$

Ⓓ $4 \times \frac{1}{2}(3 \times 4)$

Tip . . .

The logical argument in **example 2** uses a **dissection** to show that the area of the large square equals the sum of the areas of the two small squares. This verifies the Pythagorean Theorem for the specific triangle in the example.

Step-By-Step

In **example 2**, you must complete an argument to show that the Pythagorean Theorem is true for a triangle with sides of 3, 4, and 5 units.

1 The goal of this argument is to prove that $3^2 + 4^2 = 5^2$.

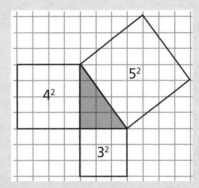

Dissect the large square into 4 triangles and 1 little square. Show that the sum of these areas is equal to 5^2, or 25.

2 Find the area of 1 triangle using the shaded triangle in the middle of the diagram. (The shaded triangle is the same size as each triangle within the large square.)

$$\frac{1}{2} \times (3 \times 4) = \boxed{}$$

3 Find the area of all 4 triangles.

$$4 \times 6 = \boxed{}$$

4 The area of the little square is 1 square unit. Add this to the areas of the 4 triangles.

$$(4 \times 6) + 1 = \boxed{}$$

5 Which answer choice matches the above equation?

1 What is the length of the hypotenuse of a right triangle with legs that are 6 centimeters and 8 centimeters?

Answer: _____

Show your work.

2 A right triangle has legs that are 8 and 15. What is the length of the hypotenuse?

Answer: _____

3 A right triangle has a hypotenuse of length 10 and one leg with length 3. What is the length of the other leg? State your answer to the nearest tenth.

Answer: _____

3 Which set of measurements will make a right triangle?

Ⓐ 5 cm, 6 cm, 11 cm

Ⓑ 9 cm, 12 cm, 16 cm

Ⓒ 7 cm, 24 cm, 25 cm

Ⓓ 12 cm, 20 cm, 25 cm

Converse of Pythagorean Theorem

If three numbers satisfy the relationship $a^2 + b^2 = c^2$, then the lengths *a, b,* and *c* can be used as the sides of a right triangle.

4 A ladder 13 ft long is placed against a wall. The ladder reaches 12 ft up the wall. How far from the wall is the bottom of the ladder?

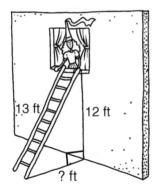

13 ft   12 ft

? ft

Ⓐ 1 ft   Ⓒ 5 ft

Ⓑ 2.5 ft   Ⓓ 25 ft

Step-By-Step

To solve **example 3**, find the numbers that satisfy the Pythagorean Theorem.

1 Start with choice Ⓐ. Square the three numbers.

$5^2 = \boxed{}$ $6^2 = \boxed{}$ $11^2 = \boxed{}$

2 Check to see if the sum of 5^2 and 6^2 equals 11^2. If it doesn't, the numbers will not make a right triangle. Write $=$ or $\neq$ in the box.

$$5^2 + 6^2 \;\boxed{}\; 11^2$$

3 Repeat steps 1 and 2 until you find the three numbers that satisfy $a^2 + b^2 = c^2$.

Think It Through

In **example 4**, use the Pythagorean Theorem to find the distance from the wall to the bottom of the ladder.

The 13-foot ladder is the hypotenuse of the right triangle formed by the floor and the wall. One side of the right triangle is 12 feet. Substitute into the formula and simplify.

$$a^2 + b^2 = c^2$$
$$12^2 + b^2 = 13^2$$
$$144 + b^2 = 169$$
$$b^2 = 169 - 144$$
$$b^2 = 25$$
$$b = \sqrt{25}$$
$$b = \boxed{}$$

 GO ON

Applying the Pythagorean Theorem

5 Katie drew a triangle to represent the shape of a poster she wants to make. She wants the poster to be in the form of a right triangle.

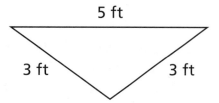

5 ft

3 ft   3 ft

Part A Is Katie's diagram a right triangle? Explain how you know.

Answer: _____

Explanation: _____

_____

_____

_____

Part B Suppose Katie wants to make a right-triangle poster with one side measuring 3 feet long and the hypotenuse measuring 5 feet long. How long should she make the other side of the triangle? Show your work.

Answer: _____

Step-By-Step

To answer **example 5**, determine if Katie drew a right triangle. Then determine the length of the third side in the triangle poster.

Part A Find out whether Katie's triangle is right by using the Pythagorean Theorem. Do her measurements fit in the formula?

$$c^2 = a^2 + b^2$$
$$c^2 = 3^2 + 3^2$$
$$c^2 = 9 + 9$$
$$c^2 = 18$$
$$c = \sqrt{18}$$
$$c \approx 4.24$$

Part B Again, use the Pythagorean Theorem to find the length of the third side.

$$c^2 = a^2 + b^2$$
$$5^2 = 3^2 + b^2$$
$$25 = 9 + b^2$$
$$b^2 = 25 - 9$$
$$b^2 = 16$$
$$b = \sqrt{16}$$
$$b = \boxed{}$$

The other side of Katie's poster is ___ feet long.

4 A 17-foot ladder leans against a wall. If the base of the ladder is 8 feet from the wall, how far up the wall is the top of the ladder?

Answer: _____

5 A diagonal brace is being used to support a wall. The brace is 25 feet long, and its base is placed 15 feet from the wall. The upper end of the brace is located four feet below the top of the wall. Make a sketch of the situation below. Label the distances. How high is the wall?

Answer: _____

6 A 7-foot-tall basketball player is designing an unusual attic whose floor, wall, and roof form a right triangle where the roof forms the hypotenuse. When he stands with his back to the wall, he wants the roof's peak to be one foot taller than he is. If he lies down along the floor, he wants his toes to be 7 feet from the point where the floor meets the roof. What should the length of the roof be to the nearest tenth of a foot?

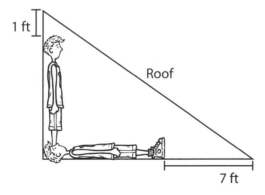

Answer: _____

GO ON

Distance and the Pythagorean Theorem

6 Sam's house is 6 miles east and 9 miles south of Amy's house.

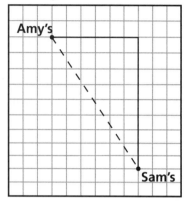

About how far is the straight-line distance from Sam's house to Amy's house?

ⓐ 3.9 mi   © 12.6 mi

ⓑ 10.8 mi   Ⓓ 15 mi

7 Find the distance between points A and B. Round to the nearest tenth.

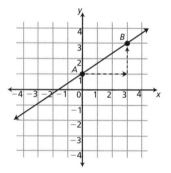

Answer: _____

Distance Formula

The distance formula allows you to find the length of a line segment on a coordinate plane using the coordinates.

If d is the distance between two points (x_1, y_1) and (x_2, y_2) in the coordinate plane, then—

$$d = \sqrt{(x_2 - x_1)^2 + (y_2 - y_1)^2}$$

Step-By-Step

Use the Pythagorean Theorem, $c^2 = a^2 + b^2$, to find the distance for **example 6**.

1 Substitute 6 miles and 9 miles for a and b in the equation.

$$c^2 = a^2 + b^2$$
$$c^2 = 6^2 + 9^2$$

2 Solve for c.

$$c^2 = 36 + 81$$
$$c^2 = 117$$
$$c = \sqrt{117}$$

$$c \approx \boxed{}$$

Step-By-Step

To solve this example, apply the Pythagorean Theorem to find the distance between the two points.

1 Draw the triangle shown with the dotted lines.

2 The two legs of the triangle have these lengths.

_____ and _____

3 Apply the Pythagorean Theorem.

$$a = 2$$
$$b = 3$$
$$c = \sqrt{(2^2 + 3^2)}$$
$$= \sqrt{4 + 9} = \sqrt{13} \approx \underline{}$$

8 Find the volume of the cone shown below. (Use 3.14 for π.)

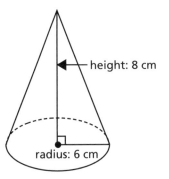

height: 8 cm

radius: 6 cm

Ⓐ 113.04 cm^3 Ⓒ 301.44 cm^3

Ⓑ 100.48 cm^3 Ⓓ 904.32 cm^3

9 The cylinder below has a radius of 2 meters and a height of 9 meters. What is the volume of the cylinder?

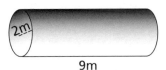

2m

9m

Ⓐ 11.13 m^3 Ⓒ 130.4 m^3

Ⓑ 113.04 m^3 Ⓓ 1,130.4 m^3

Step-By-Step

Volume is the amount of space inside a solid figure. Use the formula below to solve **example 8**.

1 Find the area of the circular base (B).

$$B = \pi r^2$$

$$\approx 3.14 \times (6)^2$$

$$\approx 3.14 \times 36 = \boxed{} \text{ cm}^2$$

2 Use B to find the volume (V).

$$V = \tfrac{1}{3}(B \times h)$$

$$\approx \tfrac{1}{3}(113.04 \times 8) = \boxed{} \text{ cm}^3$$

Step-By-Step

When the bases of a solid figure are parallel and congruent, the volume equals the area of one base times the height. In **example 9**, the base is a circle with a radius of 2 meters.

1 Find the area of one base (B).

$$B = \pi r^2$$

$$= 3.14 \times (2)^2$$

$$= 3.14 \times 4 = \boxed{} \text{ m}^2$$

2 Multiply the area of the base times the height.

$$V = 12.56 \text{ m}^2 \times 9 \text{ m} = \boxed{} \text{ m}^3$$

GO ON

Volumes of Cones, Cylinders, and Spheres

10 An artist makes globes painted with images of clouds and stars. Each globe has a diameter of 6 inches. When the artist packs a globe that she has sold, she puts it in an 8-by-8-by-8-in. box. She fills the extra space with shredded packing material.

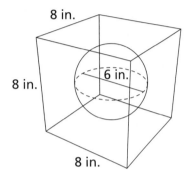

8 in.

8 in.

6 in.

8 in.

Find the volume of the space in the box that is filled with shredded packing material. Show your work and explain how you found your answer.

Answer: _____

Explanation: _____

_____

_____

_____

Step-By-Step

To solve **example 10**, you must first find the volume of the globe and the box, and then subtract the lesser volume from the greater volume.

1 Look at the *Volume Formulas* box to find the formula for determining the volume of a sphere. Use 3.14 for π. Remember that the radius is $\frac{1}{2}$ of the diameter.

$$V = \frac{4}{3}\pi r^3$$

$$V = \frac{4}{3}(3.14)(3^3)$$

$$V = \frac{4}{3}(3.14)(27)$$

$$V = \frac{4}{3}(84.78)$$

$$V \approx 113.04 \text{ in.}^3$$

2 To find the volume of the box, use the formula $V = l \times w \times h$.

$$V = l \times w \times h$$

$$V = 8 \times 8 \times 8$$

$$V = \boxed{} \text{ in.}^3$$

3 Subtract the volume of the globe from the volume of box to determine the volume of the space that is filled with packing material.

$$512 - 113.04 = \boxed{} \text{ in.}^3$$

Volume Formulas

Volume (cylinder or prism)	area of the base × height	$V = Bh$
Volume (cone or pyramid)	$\frac{1}{3}$ × area of the base × height	$V = \frac{1}{3}Bh$
Volume (sphere)	$\frac{4}{3}$ × π × radius × radius × radius	$V = \frac{4}{3}\pi r^3$

7 What is the volume of the cylinder shown. Use 3.14 for π.

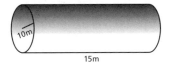

15m

Answer: _____

8 What is the volume of the object to the nearest cubic centimeter?

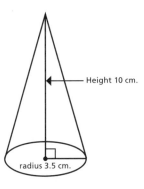

Height 10 cm.

radius 3.5 cm.

Answer: _____

9 What is the volume of a sphere with a radius of 6 cm? Round the answer to the nearest tenth.

Answer: _____

Go for it!

Test Practice 7: The Pythagorean Theorem and Volume

Estimated time: 20 minutes

Directions: Read and answer each question.

1 What is the volume of this sphere? (Use 3.14 for π.)

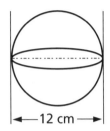

←—12 cm—→

Ⓐ 25.12 cm^3 Ⓒ 904.32 cm^3

Ⓑ 150.72 cm^3 Ⓓ $7{,}234.56 \text{ cm}^3$

2 Find the length of the missing side of the right triangle shown.

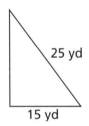

25 yd

15 yd

Ⓐ 10 yd   Ⓒ 20 yd

Ⓑ 15 yd   Ⓓ 40 yd

3 The figure shows the ramp to the loading dock at Mr. Ferguson's store. To the nearest foot, what is the length of side r of the ramp?

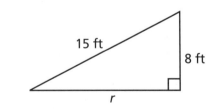

15 ft

8 ft

r

Ⓐ 7 ft   Ⓒ 17 ft

Ⓑ 13 ft   Ⓓ 161 ft

4 Darian is planting a garden in the corner of her yard. Two legs of the garden are formed by a fence and make a right angle. Their lengths are 6 ft and 8 ft. Darian needs to buy border for the hypotenuse of the triangle. Which length does she need?

Ⓐ 14 ft   Ⓒ 9 ft

Ⓑ 10 ft   Ⓓ 7.5 ft

5 A large can of paint has a diameter of 20 cm and a height of 25 cm. Which expression equals the volume of this can?

20 cm

25 cm

Ⓐ $\pi \times 10^2 \times 25$

Ⓑ $\pi \times 10 \times 25^2$

Ⓒ $\pi \times 20^2 \times 25$

Ⓓ $\pi \times 20 \times 25^2$

6 A wastepaper basket has a diameter of 12 inches and a height of 18 inches. Which expression equals the volume of the wastepaper basket?

12 in.

18 in.

Ⓐ $\pi \times 6^2 \times 18$ Ⓒ $\pi \times 12^2 \times 18$

Ⓑ $\pi \times 6 \times 18^2$ Ⓓ $\pi \times 12 \times 18^2$

7 This diagram shows that the Pythagorean Theorem is true for a triangle with sides of 5, 12, and 13.

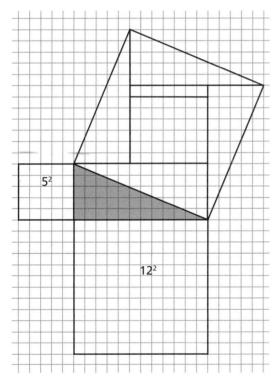

5^2

12^2

Which expression shows that the square on the hypotenuse has an area of 13^2?

Ⓐ $(\frac{1}{2} \times 5 \times 12) + 7^2$

Ⓑ $(\frac{1}{2} \times 5 \times 12) + 7$

Ⓒ $4 \times (\frac{1}{2} \times 5 \times 12) + 7$

Ⓓ $4 \times (\frac{1}{2} \times 5 \times 12) + 7^2$

8 The sphere below has a radius of 8 cm.

8 cm

What is the volume of the sphere? Round your answer to the nearest tenth. (Use 3.14 for π.)

Answer: _____

9 In line segment *AB*, point *A* is located at (3, 1) and point *B* is located at (14, 6). What is the approximate length of line segment *AB*?

Ⓐ 11

Ⓑ 12

Ⓒ 14

Ⓓ 17

10 Brian sees this tent in a catalog. He is 6 ft 2 in. tall and wants to find out if he will be able to stand up straight in the tent. What is the height of the tent?

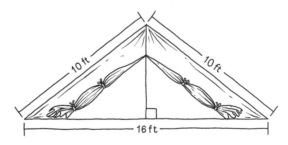

10 ft   10 ft

16 ft

Ⓐ 5 ft

Ⓑ 6 ft

Ⓒ 6.5 ft

Ⓓ 8 ft

GO ON

11 Tina is flying a kite. Her friend Grace is standing directly under the kite. How far above the ground is the kite to the nearest tenth of a foot?

Ⓐ 51.0 ft

Ⓑ 49.0 ft

Ⓒ 40.0 ft

Ⓓ 18.7 ft

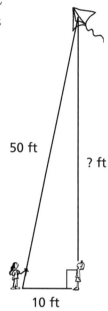

12 What is the volume of this cone? (Use 3.14 for π.)

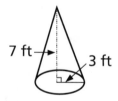

Ⓐ 43.96 ft³   Ⓒ 131.88 ft³

Ⓑ 65.94 ft³   Ⓓ 197.82 ft³

DIRECTIONS FOR QUESTION 13: Respond fully to the open-ended question that follows. Show your work and clearly explain your answer. Write your answer in the space below.

13 A rectangular garden measures 30 feet 8 inches wide and 40 feet 6 inches long. A diagonal path cuts across the garden.

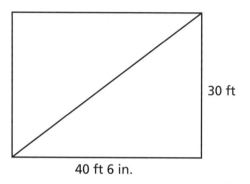

40 ft 6 in.

If Shariff walks down the diagonal and once around the garden, approximately how far will she walk? Write your answer in feet and inches.

Answer: _____

Explanation: _____

_____

_____

_____

_____

Number Correct/Total = _____/13

MATH Unit 8

Statistics and Probability

1 Scatterplots [8.SP.1]
2 Patterns of Association [8.SP.1]
3 Line of Best Fit [8.SP.2, 8.SP.3]
4 Two-Way Tables [8.SP.4]

Directions: Read and answer each question.

Scatterplots

1 Henri took a survey for his driver's education class. He had to ask several adults how many traffic tickets they had received and how many accidents they had been in as a driver. He displayed the data on the scatterplot below.

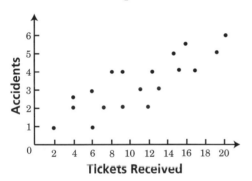

According to the data, drivers who get more tickets—

Ⓐ never have accidents.

Ⓑ have fewer accidents.

Ⓒ have more accidents.

Ⓓ always have accidents.

Step-By-Step

The graph shown in **example 1** is a scatterplot.

1 Analyze the scatterplot. Notice that the points rise as you read across the graph from left to right.

2 What happens to the number of accidents as the number of tickets received increases?

2 Darren has kept track of the time he has spent studying for tests and the scores he's received. The data are displayed in the scatterplot below.

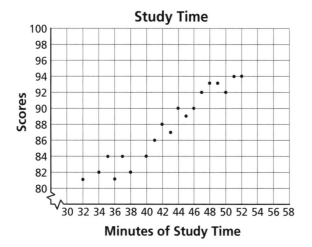

Study Time

Which best describes the correlation between Darren's study time and his grade?

Ⓐ strong positive

Ⓑ weak positive

Ⓒ negative

Ⓓ none

3 Based on the data in the scatterplot in **example 2,** predict the score Darren will receive if he studies for 55 minutes.

Ⓐ over 100

Ⓑ between 99 and 100

Ⓒ between 96 and 99

Ⓓ between 93 and 96

Think It Through

To identify the correlation between Darren's study time and his grades in **example 2,** examine the scatterplot.

If the points on the scatterplot go down from left to right, there is a *negative correlation* between the two events.

If the points go up from left to right, there is a *positive correlation* between the two events.

If the points are scattered and form no trend, there is *no relationship* between the two events.

Notice that on this scatterplot the points rise, almost in a straight line, as you read across the graph from left to right. What does this tell you about the correlation?

Think It Through

For **example 3**, the line of fit intersects 55 minutes on the graph at about 97. You can predict that Darren will get a score between 96 and 99 if he studies for 55 minutes.

Tip

A **correlation** between two data sets does not necessarily prove **causation**, or that one factor is causing another.

Interpreting Scatterplots

Positive Relationship	Negative Relationship	No Relationship
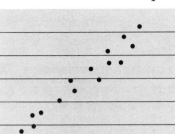	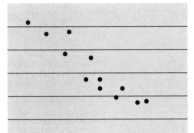	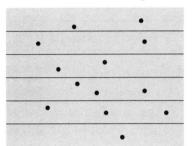

Line of Best Fit

4 Which is the line of best fit for the data shown on this graph?

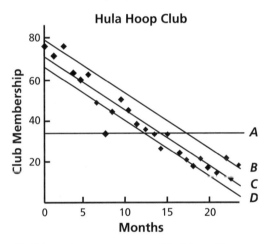

Ⓐ Line *A*   Ⓒ Line *C*

Ⓑ Line *B*   Ⓓ Line *D*

Step-By-Step

For **example 4**, recall that a line of best fit is used to show the general trend of the data on a scatterplot.

1 As time passes, the number of people in the club decreases. This is a negative correlation, so you want a line with a negative slope. One of the lines is too flat. Which one is it?

2 Look for the line where the number of dots above and below the line is nearly equal.

Remember . . .

The slope of a line shows the rate of change. In the hula hoop graph, the slope of the best fit line is negative. That shows the membership is decreasing.

Open-Ended Practice

Some tests include questions in which you must explain how you solved a problem. You may also be asked to show your work, draw graphs, or make diagrams. The example below will give you practice responding to such questions.

Line of Best Fit

5 The principal at Highwater Middle School recorded the temperature each day and the number of students absent. The scatterplot below shows his results.

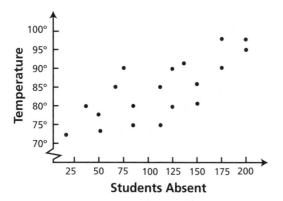

Draw a line of best fit on the scatterplot.

Which best describes the correlation between the temperature and the number of students absent: positive, negative, or no correlation? Explain how you got your answer.

Answer: _____

Explanation: _____

_____

_____

_____

_____

Step-By-Step

To solve **example 5**, first make a plan either mentally or on paper. Then show each step of your plan.

My plan: *I will draw a line of best fit on the scatterplot. Then I will use the line to describe the correlation.*

1 A **line of best fit** shows the general trend of the data on a scatterplot. To sketch a line of best fit, draw a straight line on the scatterplot so that about half the points are above the line and about half are below the line.

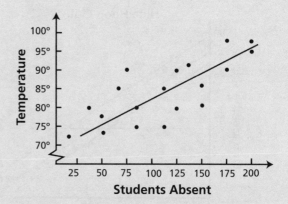

2 In short complete sentences, explain how you solved the problem, as in the example below.

I first drew a line of best fit on the graph. The line goes up as you read from left to right. This means that the number of students absent increases as the temperature increases. This shows a **positive** *correlation between temperature and absent students.*

Try It

Questions: 1–2: Use the scatterplot below.

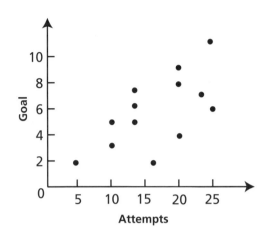

1 There is _____ correlation between attempts made and goals scored.

  Ⓐ a positive   Ⓒ no

  Ⓑ a negative

2 Draw a line of best fit. Then describe the relationship between attempts made and goals scored.

  Answer: _____

  _____

  _____

  _____

Two-Way Tables

6 One hundred 12- to 14-year-old boys and one hundred 12- to 14-year-old girls were asked, "Which after-school activities do you participate in?" The table below shows the results of the survey.

After-School Activities		
	% of boys	% of girls
Glee Club	10	25
Orchestra	40	50
Sports	65	45
Other Clubs	50	60

Which type of graph would best represent this data?

  Ⓐ bar graph

  Ⓑ double bar graph

  Ⓒ histogram

  Ⓓ circle graph

Step-By-Step

To solve **example 6**, you have to identify which type of data display would best represent the data. You are being asked to represent the difference in percentages between boys and girls and the after-school activities that they are involved in.

1 Bar graphs and histograms compare items based on a single characteristic, therefore, choices Ⓐ and Ⓒ can be eliminated.

2 A circle graph compares data, but the entire circle represents the total, or 1. Therefore, you can eliminate answer choice Ⓓ.

3 The best type of data display to compare boys and girls according to the different school activities that they participate in

  is a [_____].

Two-Way Tables

7 A health researcher collected the following data about the average heights of teenage boys and girls.

Average Height (in cm)

Age	Boys	Girls
13	157	157
14	163	161
15	168	162
16	173	162
17	175	163
18	177	164
19	180	164

Part A What does the first column of the data tell you?

_____

Part B What does the second column of the data tell you?

_____

Remember . . .
These tables are called **two-way tables** because each person is described with two variables: sex and activity or age.

Step-By-Step
To solve **example 7**, you have to identify the data shown in each column of this two-way table.

Part A The first column lists the people surveyed by ⬚⬚⬚ .

Part B The second column lists the height of the people surveyed that were ⬚⬚⬚ .

Go for it!

Test Practice 8: Statistics and Probability

Estimated time: 15 minutes

Directions: Read and answer each question.

1 The scatterplot below compares the number of car accidents in a month to the number of days of rain that month. What happens to the number of accidents as the number of rainy days increases?

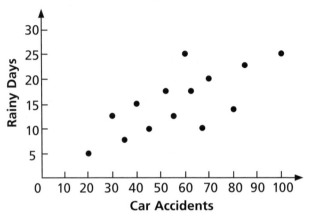

Car Accidents

- Ⓐ There is no obvious pattern.
- Ⓑ There are more accidents.
- Ⓒ There are fewer accidents.
- Ⓓ There are no accidents at all.

2

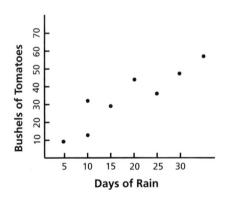

Days of Rain

Which best describes the correlation?

- Ⓐ strong positive
- Ⓑ strong negative
- Ⓒ weak negative
- Ⓓ none

3 Ms. Fletcher gave her students a vocabulary quiz at the beginning of the year. Then she polled her students asking how many books they had read over the summer. Ms. Fletcher recorded the data in the scatterplot below.

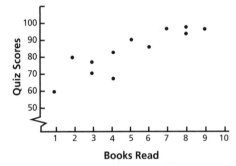

Books Read

Which describes the relationship between books read over the summer and the vocabulary quiz scores?

- Ⓐ The more books read, the higher the quiz score.
- Ⓑ The fewer books read, the higher the quiz score.
- Ⓒ The number of books read equals the quiz score.
- Ⓓ There's no relationship between the number of books read and a student's quiz score.

GO ON

4 For a science project, Nicole counted fireflies each evening. She also recorded the temperature. The data are displayed in the scatterplot below.

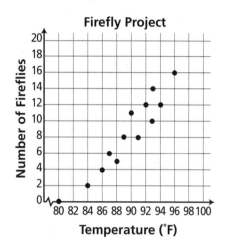

Based on the data in this scatterplot, predict the number of fireflies Nicole will see when the temperature is 100°F.

Ⓐ 8−10   Ⓒ 12−16

Ⓑ 10−12   Ⓓ 16−20

5 Which BEST describes the relationship between height and number of books read?

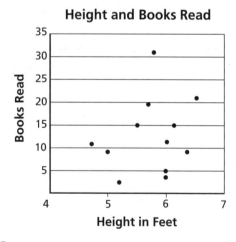

Ⓐ Height depends on the number of books read.

Ⓑ The number of books read depends on height.

Ⓒ There is no relationship between books read and height.

Ⓓ More data is needed.

6 Several students were asked if they have a computer at home and what grade they are in. Here are the survey results.

Students Answering Yes
(Grade Levels)

5 7 7 5 6 8 6 6 7 5 8 8 7 5 6 7 7 8
6 5 5 6 6 8 8 7 6 5 8 5 7 6 8 5 5
8 6 5 6 8 8 6 5 5 5 6 7 8 5 6 7 8

Students Answering No
(Grade Levels)

5 6 8 8 6 7 5 5 6 7 5 7 6 7 8 7
6 5 6 8 6 6 7 5 8 6 8 8 6 5 5

This two-way table summarizes the survey data.

What is the missing number in the table?

	Gr. 5	Gr. 6	Gr. 7	Gr. 8
Yes	15	13	10	13
No	8	10	?	7

Ⓐ 6

Ⓑ 7

Ⓒ 8

Ⓓ 10

Use the graph below to answer questions 7 and 8.

The scatterplot below compares the number of injuries during track events to the number of hours athletes practice before a competition.

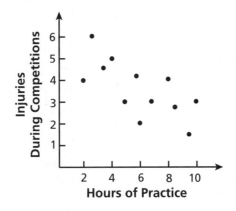

7   Which best describes the correlation between the number of injuries and the hours of practice: positive, negative, or no correlation?

Answer: _____

8   Which shows the line of best fit for the scatterplot?

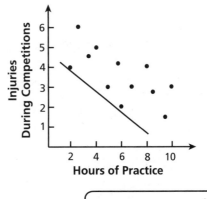

Number Correct/Total = _____/8

Mastery Test

Estimated time: 80 minutes

Directions: Read and answer each question.

1 Which number shown is closest in value to $\sqrt{445}$?

ⓐ 21 ⓒ 89

ⓑ 44 ⓓ 222

2 The value of a computer company's stock went up 150% last year. What is the decimal equivalent of 150%?

ⓐ 15.0 ⓒ 0.15

ⓑ 1.5 ⓓ 0.015

3 Which value is between $\sqrt{5}$ and $2\frac{2}{3}$?

ⓐ 1.9 ⓒ π

ⓑ $\sqrt{4}$ ⓓ 2.5

4 Which shows $0.\overline{09}$ as an equivalent fraction?

ⓐ $\frac{1}{11}$ ⓒ $\frac{9}{100}$

ⓑ $\frac{1}{101}$ ⓓ $\frac{9}{10}$

5 Which statement is false?

ⓐ $\sqrt{7} < 2.8$

ⓑ $-\frac{7}{9} < -0.72$

ⓒ $3\frac{1}{2} < \sqrt{260}$

ⓓ $\pi < 2\frac{5}{8}$

6 Which of the following is an irrational number?

ⓐ $\sqrt{11}$ ⓒ $-\frac{17}{3}$

ⓑ 225 ⓓ 0.4545 . . .

7 Which of these is NOT a rational number?

ⓐ $4\frac{1}{3}$ ⓒ $\sqrt{5}$

ⓑ $\frac{3}{5}$ ⓓ 14

8 Show that 3.1 is a rational number by writing it as the ratio of two integers.

ⓐ $\frac{1}{3}$

ⓑ $\frac{10}{31}$

ⓒ $\frac{31}{10}$

ⓓ $\frac{31}{100}$

9 Which answer choice shows 0.00000001059 in scientific notation?

ⓐ 10.59×10^7 ⓒ 1.059×10^8

ⓑ 1.059×10^{-8} ⓓ 0.1059×10^7

10 Find $\sqrt{576}$.

ⓐ 36 ⓒ 21

ⓑ 24 ⓓ 18

11 What is the value of 64^2?

ⓐ 8 ⓒ 496

ⓑ 128 ⓓ 4,096

12 Which answer shows 54,000,000 written in scientific notation?

ⓐ 5.4×10^8 ⓒ 5.4×10^{-7}

ⓑ 5.4×10^7 ⓓ 5.4×10^{-8}

13 Simplify.

$$\frac{(4^4 \times 4^9)}{4^{15}}$$

ⓐ $\frac{1}{4^2}$ ⓒ 4

ⓑ $\frac{1}{4}$ ⓓ 4^2

14 $(12^3)(12^2) =$

 Ⓐ 12^5 Ⓒ 144^5

 Ⓑ 12^6 Ⓓ 144^6

15 The area of a square is 144 cm^2. What is the perimeter of the square?

 Ⓐ 12 cm   Ⓒ 72 cm

 Ⓑ 48 cm   Ⓓ 288 cm

16 What is the slope of this line?

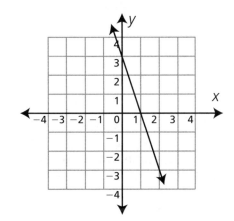

 Ⓐ -3 Ⓒ $\frac{1}{3}$

 Ⓑ $-\frac{1}{3}$ Ⓓ 3

17 Ellen's average bike speed is 220 yards per minute. How long will it take her to bike a distance of 3 miles? (1 mi = 1,760 yd)

 Ⓐ 8 min   Ⓒ 72 min

 Ⓑ 24 min   Ⓓ 73 min

18 Oranges are 5 pounds for $3.35. Which proportion can be used to find the cost of 8 pounds of oranges?

 Ⓐ $\frac{5}{3.35} = \frac{c}{8}$

 Ⓑ $\frac{5}{3.35} = \frac{c}{13}$

 Ⓒ $\frac{5}{3.35} = \frac{8}{c}$

 Ⓓ $\frac{5}{8} = \frac{c}{3.35}$

19 The table compares the number of loaves of bread Emile makes to the amount of flour he uses.

Loaves	Flour (lbs)
3	5
6	10
9	15
12	20

Which is the BEST description of the pattern?

 Ⓐ For every 3 loaves of bread, Emile uses 1 pound of flour.

 Ⓑ For every 5 loaves of bread, Emile uses 1 pound of flour.

 Ⓒ For every 3 loaves of bread, Emile uses 5 pounds of flour.

 Ⓓ For every 5 loaves of bread, Emile uses 3 pounds of flour.

20 What is the equation of this line?

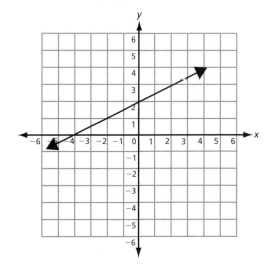

 Ⓐ $y = 2x + 2$

 Ⓑ $y = -4x + 2$

 Ⓒ $y = \frac{1}{2}x + 2$

 Ⓓ $y = \frac{1}{2}x - 4$

GO ON

21 Which is the graph for $y = \frac{1}{2}x + 3$?

Ⓐ

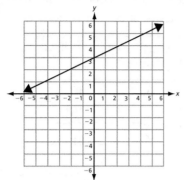

Ⓑ

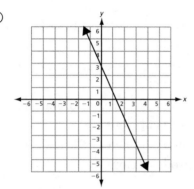

Ⓒ

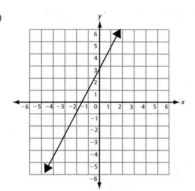

Ⓓ

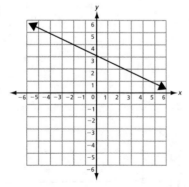

22 What is the y-intercept of this graph?

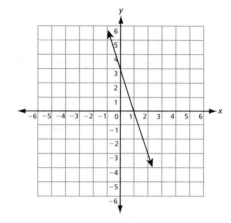

Ⓐ $\frac{1}{3}$

Ⓑ -3

Ⓒ $-\frac{1}{3}$

Ⓓ 3

23 Which equation shows a line that passes through the origin?

Ⓐ $y = x + 4$

Ⓑ $y = x - 4$

Ⓒ $y = 4 - x$

Ⓓ $y = -4x$

24 Find the value of y in the equation below.

$$3y + 7 = -14$$

Ⓐ $y = -21$ Ⓒ $y = -\frac{7}{3}$

Ⓑ $y = -7$ Ⓓ $y = 7$

25 Solve this system by graphing.

$$2y - x = 7$$
$$2x + 3y = 0$$

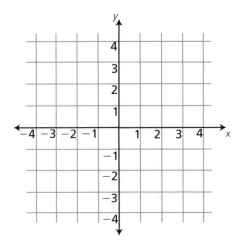

Ⓐ $(-3, 2)$ Ⓒ $(1, 4)$
Ⓑ $(0, 0)$ Ⓓ $(3, -2)$

26 Solve $3(2y - 1) = 8 + y$.

Ⓐ $y = -1.4$ Ⓒ $y = 1.8$
Ⓑ $y = -1$ Ⓓ $y = 2.2$

27 How many solutions does this equation have?

$$2(5 - x) + 3 = -15 - 2x$$

Ⓐ 0
Ⓑ 1
Ⓒ 2
Ⓓ an infinite number

28 Which ordered pair is the solution to this system of equations?

$$2x - y = 5$$
$$x + y = 4$$

Ⓐ $(-3, -1)$ Ⓒ $(3, 1)$
Ⓑ $(-1, -3)$ Ⓓ $(1, 3)$

29 Choose the system of equations that represents the problem situation below.

The perimeter of a rectangle is 32 inches. It is 3 times as long as it is wide.

Ⓐ $x + y = 32$
    $3x = y$
Ⓑ $x + y = 32$
    $3 + x = y$
Ⓒ $2x + 2y = 32$
    $3 + x = y$
Ⓓ $2x + 2y = 32$
    $3x = y$

30 A system of two linear equations has no solution. What must be true of the graphs of these equations?

Ⓐ The lines are parallel.
Ⓑ The lines are identical.
Ⓒ The line are perpendicular.
Ⓓ The lines intersect in exactly one point.

31 Which equation shows the relationship between x and y?

x	y
−2	−4
−1	−1
0	2
1	5

Ⓐ $y = 3x + 2$
Ⓑ $y = 2x$
Ⓒ $y = x - 2$
Ⓓ $y = x$

GO ON

32 Which is the graph for this function?

x	−4	−2	0	2
y	0	1	2	3

Ⓐ

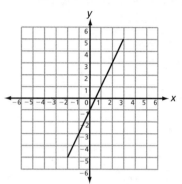

Ⓑ

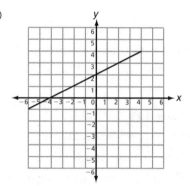

Ⓒ

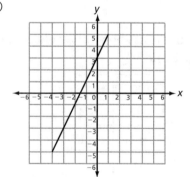

Ⓓ

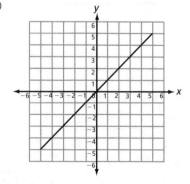

33 Which is the graph of a linear function?

Ⓐ

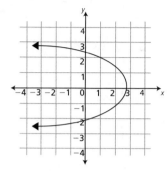

Ⓑ

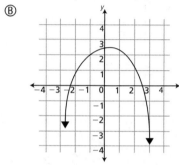

Ⓒ

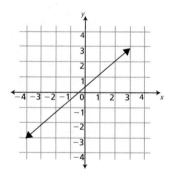

Ⓓ

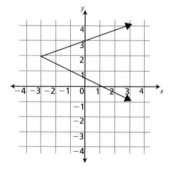

34 What relationship is shown by the ordered pairs in this table?

x	y
2	−1
4	3
0	1
2	1

Ⓐ function that is not a relation

Ⓑ relation that is not a function

Ⓒ both a function and a relation

Ⓓ neither a function nor a relation

35 Which set of ordered pairs is not a function?

Ⓐ {(1, 0), (2, 1), (3, 2), (4, 3)}

Ⓑ {(1, 0), (2, 1), (1, 2), (2, 3)}

Ⓒ {(0, 1), (2, 1), (3, 1), (1, 1)}

Ⓓ {(1, 1), (2, 2), (3, 3), (4, 4)}

36 The sum of Roy's age and Catherine's age is 29. Catherine is one year older than Roy. If r represents Roy's age, which equation can be used to find Roy's age?

Ⓐ $r + (r + 1) = 29$

Ⓑ $29 - 1 = r$

Ⓒ $(r - 1) + r = 29$

Ⓓ $29 \div 2 - 1 = r$

37 This graph shows a function that models the speed of a moving object. For what values of the time, x, is this function increasing?

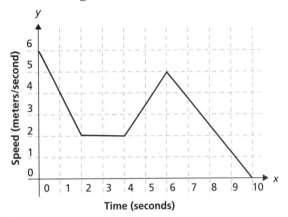

Ⓐ $0 \leq x \leq 2$ Ⓒ $4 \leq x \leq 6$

Ⓑ $2 \leq x \leq 6$ Ⓓ $6 \leq x \leq 10$

38 Plot the following points on the coordinate grid. Connect the points in order to form a quadrilateral.

$(-3, -1), (-2, -3), (2, -3), (1, -1)$

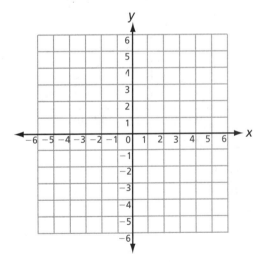

Reflect the quadrilateral over the x-axis. Which ordered pair is one of the vertices of the new figure?

Ⓐ $(3, -2)$ Ⓒ $(1, 3)$

Ⓑ $(3, 2)$ Ⓓ $(1, 1)$

GO ON

39 If figure *ABCDE* is rotated 180°
counterclockwise on vertex *B*, which point
will be a coordinate of the rotated figure?

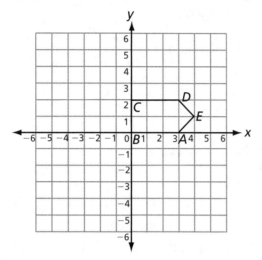

Ⓐ (−4, −1)   Ⓒ (−2, 0)

Ⓑ (−1, −3)   Ⓓ (−4, 1)

40 Determine the length of *x* in the pair of
similar right triangles.

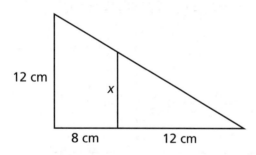

Ⓐ 7.2 cm

Ⓑ 7.5 cm

Ⓒ 18 cm

Ⓓ 20 cm

41 In the figure, *m* and *n* are parallel lines.
Angle 2 has a measure of 100°. What is
the measure of angle 5?

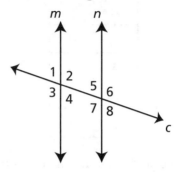

Ⓐ 260°   Ⓒ 100°

Ⓑ 180°   Ⓓ 80°

42 The endpoints of $\overline{JK}$ are *J*(−1, 2)
and *K*(3, 2). $\overline{JK}$ is enlarged by a scale
factor of 2 to form $\overline{J'K'}$. Which are the
possible coordinates of $\overline{J'K'}$? The origin is
used as the center of the dilation.

Ⓐ *J*′(−2, 2), *K*′(6, 2)

Ⓑ *J*′(−2, 4), *K*′(6, 4)

Ⓒ *J*′(1, 2), *K*′(5, 2)

Ⓓ *J*′(−1, 4), *K*′(3, 4)

43 Figures *ABCD* and *RSTV* are congruent.
What is the measure of ∠*STV*?

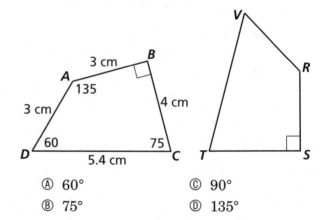

Ⓐ 60°   Ⓒ 90°

Ⓑ 75°   Ⓓ 135°

44 In △*DEF*, two angles each measure 35°. What is the measure of the third angle?

   Ⓐ 55°   Ⓒ 135°

   Ⓑ 110°   Ⓓ 145°

45 Which transformation is shown by this pair of triangles?

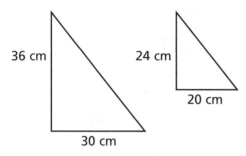

   Ⓐ horizontal translation

   Ⓑ dilation by a factor of $\frac{2}{3}$

   Ⓒ dilation by a factor of $\frac{1}{2}$

   Ⓓ dilation by a factor of 2

46 What is the measure of ∠*PCB* ?

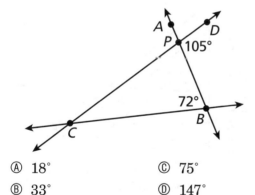

   Ⓐ 18°   Ⓒ 75°

   Ⓑ 33°   Ⓓ 147°

47 Trapezoid *ABCD* is reflected across the *x*-axis and then rotated 90° clockwise. The result is labeled *PQRS*. What must be true of *PQRS*?

   Ⓐ It has right angles.

   Ⓑ It has two congruent sides.

   Ⓒ It has one pair of parallel sides.

   Ⓓ Its area is smaller than the area of *ABCD*.

48 Benita created a new game that uses a game board shaped like a right triangle. If the two shorter sides are 9 in. and 12 in., what is the measure of the third side?

   Ⓐ 12 in.

   Ⓑ 15 in.

   Ⓒ 16 in.

   Ⓓ 18 in.

49 A water storage tank, in the shape of a cylinder, has a diameter of 20 meters and a height of 50 meters. Which expression equals the volume of this tank?

   Ⓐ $\pi \times 10^2 \times 50$

   Ⓑ $\pi \times 10 \times 50^2$

   Ⓒ $\pi \times 20^2 \times 50$

   Ⓓ $\pi \times 20 \times 50^2$

50 Nell made a patch to sew on her backpack. The shape of the patch is a right triangle. What is the length of the base to the nearest tenth of a centimeter?

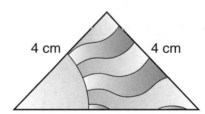

   Ⓐ 6.1 cm

   Ⓑ 6.0 cm

   Ⓒ 5.7 cm

   Ⓓ 4.7 cm

GO ON ⇨

51 To the nearest cubic centimeter, what is the volume of a ball with a radius of 4 centimeters? (Use 3.14 for π.)

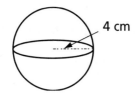

4 cm

Ⓐ 33 cm^3

Ⓑ 67 cm^3

Ⓒ 201 cm^3

Ⓓ 268 cm^3

52 Which set of measurements can be used to make a right triangle?

Ⓐ 7 cm, 20 cm, 24 cm

Ⓑ 9 cm, 40 cm, 41 cm

Ⓒ 10 cm, 24 cm, 25 cm

Ⓓ 12 cm, 35 cm, 38 cm

53 What is the distance from point P at $(-15, -4)$ to point Q at $(-8, 20)$?

Answer: _____

54 Dana recorded the number of rainy days each week and the number of days her gym class met outside. The scatterplot below shows her data. What is the relationship between the two sets of data?

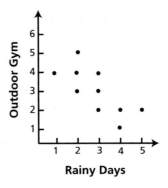

Ⓐ none

Ⓑ strong negative

Ⓒ weak positive

Ⓓ strong positive

55 Which is the line of best fit for the data shown on this graph?

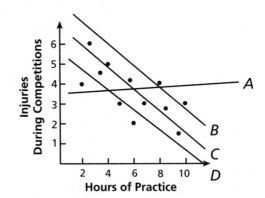

Ⓐ line A Ⓒ line C

Ⓑ line B Ⓓ line D

56 Robin started a savings account with $50. She made this scatterplot of her savings.

Savings Account Balance

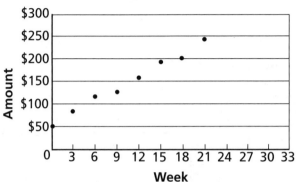

According to the scatterplot, when will Robin have saved $300?

Ⓐ about week 21

Ⓑ about week 24

Ⓒ about week 27

Ⓓ about week 33

57 What relationship is suggested by this scatterplot?

Sandwiches Sold

Ⓐ The lower the price, the fewer sandwiches sold.

Ⓑ The lower the price, the more sandwiches sold.

Ⓒ The more sandwiches sold, the higher the price.

Ⓓ The price is not related to the number of sandwiches sold.

58 Blue Lake Junior High is selling raffle tickets to pave the parking lot. The tickets sell for $1, $5, or $10. Here are the sales by grade level.

Grade 7 Tickets Sold (Dollar Amounts)											
1	5	1	5	1	10	1	1	10	1	5	
5	1	10	1	5	10	5	10	5	1	1	
1	5	10	5	1	1	10	1	5	1		

Grade 8 Tickets Sold (Dollar Amounts)											
5	10	1	5	1	1	5	5	10	1	1	
1	10	1	5	10	5	10	5	1	10	5	
5	1	10	10	1	1	5	1	5	1		

This two-way table summarizes the ticket sales. What is the missing number?

	$1	**$5**	**$10**
Grade 7	15	10	7
Grade 8	13	?	8

Ⓐ 10

Ⓑ 11

Ⓒ 12

Ⓓ 13

Number Correct/Total = _____/58

Common Core Math 8

Keeping Score

	Points Earned / Total Points	Percent Score
Tryout Test	/58	%
Test Practice 1 The Number System	/15	%
Test Practice 2 Radicals and Integer Exponents	/20	%
Test Practice 3 Proportional Relationships	/15	%
Test Practice 4 Linear Equations and Systems	/14	%
Test Practice 5 Functions	/20	%
Test Practice 6 Geometry	/25	%
Test Practice 7 The Pythagorean Theorem and Volume	/13	%
Test Practice 8 Statistics	/8	%
Mastery Test	/58	%

1. Fill in the number of points you earned in the Points Earned box.

2. Use the Finding Percent chart on page 125 to figure out your Percent Score. Then fill in the % box.

3. Compare your Percent Scores for the Tryout Test and the Mastery Test. See how much you've learned!

Finding Percent

Many tests give your score in both number of points earned and in percentages. This handy chart will tell you your percent score.

1. Find the band with the same number of points that are on your test.
2. Follow along the top row of the band to the number of points you earned. Your percent score is right below it.

Number of Questions on Test

8

1	2	3	4	5	6	7	8
13%	25%	38%	50%	63%	75%	88%	100%

13

1	2	3	4	5	6	7	8	9	10	11	12	13
8%	15%	23%	31%	38%	46%	54%	62%	69%	77%	85%	92%	100%

14

1	2	3	4	5	6	7	8	9	10	11	12	13	14
7%	14%	21%	29%	36%	43%	50%	57%	64%	71%	79%	86%	93%	100%

15

1	2	3	4	5	6	7	8	9	10	11	12	13	14	15
7%	13%	20%	27%	33%	40%	47%	53%	60%	67%	73%	80%	87%	93%	100%

20

1	2	3	4	5	6	7	8	9	10	11	12	13	14	15	16	17	18	19	20
5%	10%	15%	20%	25%	30%	35%	40%	45%	50%	55%	60%	65%	70%	75%	80%	85%	90%	95%	100%

25

1	2	3	4	5	6	7	8	9	10	11	12	13	14	15	16	17	18	19	20
4%	8%	12%	16%	20%	24%	28%	32%	36%	40%	44%	48%	52%	56%	60%	64%	68%	72%	76%	80%

21	22	23	24	25
84%	88%	92%	96%	100%

58

1	2	3	4	5	6	7	8	9	10	11	12	13	14	15	16	17	18	19	20
2%	3%	5%	7%	9%	10%	12%	14%	16%	17%	19%	21%	22%	24%	26%	28%	29%	31%	33%	34%

21	22	23	24	25	26	27	28	29	30	31	32	33	34	35	36	37	38	39	40
36%	38%	40%	41%	43%	45%	47%	48%	50%	52%	53%	55%	57%	59%	60%	62%	64%	66%	67%	69%

41	42	43	44	45	46	47	48	49	50	51	52	53	54	55	56	57	58
71%	72%	74%	76%	78%	79%	81%	83%	84%	86%	88%	90%	91%	93%	95%	97%	98%	100%